Black and Brown Bear Activity at Selected Coastal Sites in Glacier Bay National Park and Preserve, Alaska: A Preliminary Assessment Using Noninvasive Procedures

By Steve Partridge and Tom Smith, U.S. Geological Survey, and Tania Lewis National Park Service

Prepared in cooperation with the National Park Service

Open-File Report 2009-1169

U.S. Department of the Interior
U.S. Geological Survey

U.S. Department of the Interior
KEN SALAZAR, Secretary

U.S. Geological Survey
Suzette Kimball, Acting Director

U.S. Geological Survey, Reston, Virginia: 2009

For more information on the USGS—the Federal source for science about the Earth, its natural and living resources, natural hazards, and the environment, visit http://www.usgs.gov or call 1-888-ASK-USGS.

For an overview of USGS information products, including maps, imagery, and publications, visit http://www.usgs.gov/pubprod

To order this and other USGS information products, visit http://store.usgs.gov

Suggested citation:
Partridge, Steve, Smith, Tom, and Lewis, Tania, 2009, Black and brown bear activity at selected coastal sites in Glacier Bay National Park and Preserve, Alaska: A preliminary assessment using noninvasive procedures: U.S. Geological Survey Open-File Report 2009-1169, 62 p.

Contents

Figures

Tables

Conversion Factors, Abbreviations, and Acronyms

Multiply	By	To obtain
decimeter (dm)	3.937	inch (in)
meter (m)	3.281	foot (ft)
square kilometer (km^2)	0.3861	square mile (mi^2)
liter (L)	0.2642	gallon (gal)
kilogram (kg)	2.205	pound avoirdupois (lb)

Inch/Pound to SI

Multiply	By	To obtain
mile (mi)	1.609	kilometer (km)

Abbreviations, Acronyms, and Symbols	Meaning
BFDI	Bear forage diversity index
DNA	Deoxyribonucleic acid
GLBA	Glacier Bay National Park and Preserve
GIS	Geographic Information System
GPS	Global Positioning System
mtDNA	Mitochondrial deoxyribonucleic acid
nDNA	Nuclear deoxyribonucleic acid
NPS	National Park Service
USGS	U. S. Geological Survey

Black and Brown Bear Activity at Selected Coastal Sites in Glacier Bay National Park and Preserve, Alaska: A Preliminary Assessment Using Noninvasive Procedures

By Steve Partridge[1], Tom Smith[2], and Tania Lewis[3]

Abstract

A number of efforts in recent years have sought to predict bear activity in various habitats to minimize human disturbance and bear/human conflicts. Alaskan coastal areas provide important foraging areas for bears (*Ursus americanus* and *U. arctos*), particularly following den emergence when there may be no snow-free foraging alternatives. Additionally, coastal areas provide important food items for bears throughout the year. Glacier Bay National Park and Preserve (GLBA) in southeastern Alaska has extensive coastal habitats, and the National Park Service (NPS) has been long interested in learning more about the use of these coastal habitats by bears because these same habitats receive extensive human use by park visitors, especially kayaking recreationists. This study provides insight regarding the nature and intensity of bear activity at selected coastal sites within GLBA. We achieved a clearer understanding of bear/habitat relationships within GLBA by analyzing bear activity data collected with remote cameras, bear sign mapping, scat collections, and genetic analysis of bear hair.

Although we could not quantify actual levels of bear activity at study sites, agreement among measures of activity (for example, sign counts, DNA analysis, and video record) lends support to our qualitative site assessments. This work suggests that habitat evaluation, bear sign mapping, and periodic scat counts can provide a useful index of bear activity for sites of interest.

---

[1]U.S. Geological Survey Alaska Science Center Anchorage, AK 99508 Present Address: 704 Piltz Court, Hood River, OR 97031

[2]U.S. Geological Survey Alaska Science Center, Anchorage, AK 99508 Present Address: Brigham Young University, Department of Plant and Wildlife Sciences, 451 WIDB-BYU Provo, Utah 84602

[3]National Park Service, Glacier Bay National Park & Preserve, Gustavus, AK 99826

Introduction

Alaskan coastal areas provide important foraging areas for bears (*Ursus americanus* and *U. arctos*), particularly following den emergence when there may be no snow-free foraging alternatives (Vequist, 1989; Smith and Partridge, 2004). Glacier Bay National Park and Preserve (GLBA) in southeastern Alaska (fig. 2) has extensive coastal habitats, and the National Park Service (NPS) was interested in learning more about the use of these coastal habitats by bears because these same habitats also receive extensive human use by park visitors, especially kayakers. Due to the steep ruggedness of surrounding topography, as well as easy water access, kayakers favor beaches for kayak haul-out and camping. Consequently, people and bears frequently encounter one another. Potentially dangerous bear encounters (involving contact or property destruction) seasonally occur (T. Smith, Brigham Young University, Provo, Utah. unpub. data, 2002YEAR; Lewis and others, 2006; fig. 1). To address its dual mandate of protecting the natural environment as well as providing visitor access, park managers need information regarding bear habitat use to help advance visitor safety as well as reduce disturbance to bears. Here, we present findings of a study conducted from 2004 to 2005 to investigate bear activity levels within selected sites along coastal regions within GLBA.

The nutritional status of bears, particularly females, is related to parameters affecting individual and population productivity (Samson and Huot, 1995; Hilderbrand and others, 1999). Consequently, seasonal differences in bear use should track the temporal and spatial changes in nutrient availability across habitats. There are several ways to address habitat quality as it relates to selection of habitats by bears. Qualitative analysis of habitat characteristics has been used by several researchers (MacHutcheon and Wellwood, 2003; Smith and others, written commun., 2002, Brigham Young University, Provo, Utah) to address bear use or bear encounter potential. The assumption underlying these studies is that as habitat quality increases, bear use and the probability of bear/human encounters also increases. Although qualitative measures may prove appropriate for evaluating bear use patterns, they have yet to be compared to actual bear activity data to test their predictive effectiveness.

Quantitative habitat assessment also has been used to evaluate bear use (Hamilton and Bunnell, 1987). Hamilton and Bunnell (1987) found that one of the two females they closely monitored appeared to be foraging optimally (maximizing energy intake per unit time), although one female? did not follow this pattern. Monitoring the selection and activity of individual animals has many advantages, but may not directly reflect activity patterns on a population level. Habitat selection, especially among females, will vary among years depending on the reproductive status of the bear as well as other factors, such as the presence of other bears and the variable quality and quantity of forage across habitats (Weilgus and Bunnell, 1994, 2000). Thus, some bears during certain time periods may forgo optimal foraging opportunities in an effort to protect offspring by avoiding other bears. For example, during a 2-year study in Kenai Fjords National Park, females with dependent offspring were encountered in beach habitats only twice in areas with high black bear densities (Smith and others, unpub. data, 2004, Brigham Young University, Provo, Utah.). Black bears also may change their activity patterns if sympatric with grizzly bears (Holm and others, 1999; Jacoby and others, 1999). Given these complications, monitoring productive areas for overall bear use may be preferable to using individual animals whose habitat selection may be highly variable between years. This habitat-centric approach also meshes better with current information needs because management activities generally are focused on specific sites, not individual animals.

Knowledge of bears' habitat use patterns is relevant to many management issues and helps reduce risks associated with camping in bear habitat. Due to the relatively low densities and the cryptic nature of bears, remote photography has proven to be a valuable tool for documenting bear activity (Mace and others, 1994; MacHutchon and others, 1998). Time-lapse remote photography can provide a measure of overall use and activity rates. Still cameras coupled with infrared detectors can be used to monitor use of smaller areas of interest (for example, well established bear trails, river corridors, and bear mark-trees). In addition to these means of monitoring bear activity, other habitat features affect bear use. For example, the presence of productive beach habitats, adjacent foraging areas, and travel corridors influence levels of bear activity in any given area.

The recent use of noninvasive genetic sampling in wildlife research has increased substantially (Waits and others, 2001; Waits and Paetkau, 2005). Mitochondrial DNA (mtDNA) fragments can be useful in identifying bear species, and specific fragments of nuclear DNA (nDNA) can be used to identify the unique genotypes of individual bears (Waits and others, 2001). Local bear density in an undisturbed unhunted area largely is a result of factors relating to habitat quality (Gilbert and Lanner, 1995). Thus, bear numbers likely reflect habitat quality. Obtaining a measure of the minimum number of individual bears in selected study sites will provide an additional measure of habitat use and quality. Additionally, determining the relative distribution of black and brown bears within study sites is important because encounters with brown bears generally are much more dangerous than those with black bears (Herrero, 2002).

Research Objectives

The NPS requested the USGS to undertake this study using methods that did not involve the capture and handling of bears to place radio collars on them. Thus, the primary objective was to determine the degree to which habitat characteristics at selected study sites are predictive of bear activity. We approached this research objective with four subtasks.

1. Assess bear temporal and spatial use of selected sites within GLBA with remote cameras and direct observation.
    a. Use remote cameras to determine bear activity rates and the temporal, spatial, and numerical activity patterns of bears within selected sites in GLBA.
    b. Opportunistically record bear activity by direct observation.
    c. Document fresh bear sign over time.
2. Habitat mapping and evaluation.
    a. Use systematic sampling procedures to map important bear forage resources, including species composition and biomass.
    b. Track the phenology of key bear forage species.
    c. Use Geographic Information Systems (GIS) to incorporate larger scale habitat features into an overall habitat assessment model.
3. Bear nutritional ecology.
    a. Collect important bear forage items for nutritional analysis.
    b. Directly observe foraging bears to estimate intake rates for selected forages.
    c. Use bear hair collected from snares and mark trees to run stable isotope analyses.
    d. Collect and analyze fresh bear scats to determine relative seasonal importance of bear foods.

4. Bear distribution and minimum numbers

    a. Collect a sampling of bear hair and use molecular genetic analysis to determine the minimum bear numbers and species using a given site.

Besides using results from this work to validate bear/habitat relationships estimated by Smith and others (written commun., Brigham Young University, Provo, Utah 2006), results also will provide input to the bear management and backcountry management plans for GLBA. Results of this research will aid GLBA managers by providing the following information:

1. A profile of the spatial and temporal use of selected sites by black and brown bears;

2. An evaluation of the appropriateness of using site specific and landscape-level parameters to estimate seasonal bear activity rates;

3. A seasonal nutritional profile for bears using selected sites;

4. A minimum number of bears using selected sites as well as distribution of black and brown bears within these sites, an evaluation of camping closure areas (for example, Tarr Inlet and Sandy Cove) in relation to other selected sites with regard their bear habitat potential; and

5. A profile of seasonally important bear forage items.

Methods

Study Site Selection

Eight sites were selected within GLBA for study in summers 2004–05 (fig. 2). Study site selections were based on several criteria. First, we included several areas within Tarr and Johns Hopkins Inlets, and Sandy Cove because they have been closed to camping for more than two decades following a series of bear/human conflicts and were of special interest to management. Russell Passage, Queen and Reid Inlets, and Tlingit and Wolf Points were selected due to historically high levels of bear activity and/or human/bear encounters. As a result, most study sites were located in the West Arm of Glacier Bay. Other factors, such as the extent of the view-shed for remote camera monitoring use, also helped guide study site selection in the broader context of the previous criteria. Study sites extended from the beach/ocean interface inland to a line parallel to the beach and 50 m beyond the edge of dense closed scrub or needle leaf forest.

We restricted our analysis to this narrow band of coast because (a) the primary overlap of bear and human activity was presumed to occur within this narrow band, (b) steep topography in many instances is encountered at this point and both bear and human use were presumed to decrease substantially at that point, and (c) dense alder and/or needle leaf forests were presumed to offer little forage for bears and to be difficult for bears to traverse.

Site Visits

Each study site was visited seven times annually from early June to late August. On the first site visit, all research equipment was installed, including remote video cameras and hair snare traps. During each visit, vegetation communities and existing bear sign were mapped. All bear scats were analyzed for gross content and scattered to avoid recounting. Hair samples were removed from barb-wire snares and rub trees and stored. Sites were visited at 2-week intervals and video camera cassette tapes were replaced, new scats analyzed and scattered, and hair samples collected. Although we could not visit every site in 1 field day, the visitation dates did not differ by more than 3–4 days between and deemed a single round of site visits (table 1).

A checklist of probable bear forage plants was kept and notes regarding the phenology of those plants were recorded. In addition, we followed bear foraging trails and noted which plants were fed upon. Foraging trails were evident by trampled vegetation, tracks and sign of recent grazing (for example, cut stems, digs, and cropped grasses). Upon completion of an area sweep for signs of bear activity, we continued vegetation and habitat mapping.

Study Site Vegetation Mapping

All study sites were mapped using handheld Global Positioning System (GPS) equipment (Trimble GeoExplorer 3®, Trimble Navigation Limited, Sunnyvale, CA, USA), GIS software (ESRI ArcGIS 9.x, Redlands, CA, USA), and existing imagery. Vegetation classes were defined in the field based on characteristics provided by Viereck (1992; appendix 1). Vegetation mapping and analyses followed the methods of Daubenmire (1959). A 2 × 5 dm sampling square (fig. 3) was used in all habitats with the exception of closed scrub or forest, where a 1 × 1 m plot was used. A target number of 40 plots per habitat type per year across all study sites was set to describe species composition. A larger plot size (forty 10 × 10 m plots per type) was used to describe scrub vegetation. Our approach to vegetation sampling was a stratified random approach. Transects were stratified within habitats and points along those transects were randomly selected. However, scrub vegetation plots were established along randomly located transects. Whenever the average width of scrub vegetation was ≤ 15 m, one Daubenmire plot per transect provided an estimate of foliar coverage. If the average width was > 15 m but < 50 m, two plots per transect were used, and if > 50 m, three plots per transect were used. Plot placement along transects was determined with a random numbers table. Random numbers identified the distance from the beginning of the transect at which the plot would be placed.

Bear Sign Assessment

We surveyed each site during each visit for bear sign by walking parallel transects that provided a thorough view of each study site. Transect spacing varied according to site visibility: transects were farther apart in open areas and closer when terrain and/or vegetation were limiting. When bear sign was encountered (for example, bear scat, rub trees, chew logs, bear beds, mark trails, foraging trails, bear tracks, and areas of bear digging), the type and location were recorded on a GPS. As previously described, a gross analysis of scat content was conducted (that is, vegetation, bone, hair, etc.) and scats were scattered so as to not be counted on subsequent visits. Bear mark trails and mark trees (sometimes called rub trees) were photographed and hairs on rub trees collected. All data from bear sign surveys were placed in GIS for display and subsequent analysis (fig. 4).

Hair Collection and DNA Analysis

Bear hairs were collected within study sites by several methods. We installed one baited barbed-wire hair trap within each study site (fig. 5). Hair snare placements were situated: (1) about 100 m from the beach, (2) in areas that were not easily accessible by kayak/campers, and (3) in areas accessible by bears. Hair snares consisted of a single strand of barbed-wire tightly wound around three or more tree trunks or wooden fence posts, thus creating a triangular enclosure. Wire placement was about 0.5 m above the ground. Each trap was marked with fluorescent survey flagging and signs to alert campers of the bait station's presence. We piled loose rocks, branches, moss, or other debris within each enclosure, then doused them with a liter of scent-bait. Scent-bait was a mixture of fetid cows' blood, fish oil, skunk oil, and glycerol. Biweekly we carefully checked each enclosure for hairs, and then recharged scent with a liter of scent-bait. We used a small butane pocket-torch to clear barbs of hairs once a few had been pulled for subsequent analysis. To augment hair collection, we selected one rub tree per study site, attached a small piece of barbed wire to its trunk, and checked them for hairs during biweekly visits (fig. 6). Additionally, we opportunistically collected bear hair from rub logs and vegetation along trails. All hairs with follicles were placed in small paper envelopes and stored in desiccant to preserve them for later analysis. Hair samples were categorized as fresh (caught on the wire since the last site visit), old (opportunistic hair samples that appeared to have been there for several weeks or longer), or unknown (if age was indeterminable). We categorized the apparent age of hair samples for prioritization of sample analysis because funds for genetic analysis were limited. The relative quality of hair samples also was recorded: >10 individual hairs or samples with guard hairs with follicles were rated as high; those with 7–9 individual hairs were rated as moderate; those that contained 5–6 individual hairs, or with a high proportion of under fur, were rated as low quality; samples with < 5 individual hairs were not collected.

We analyzed the DNA in a subset of the hair samples collected in 2005 to identify individual bears. We used several criteria to determine which hair samples would be analyzed. Initially, we excluded hair samples categorized as old or of unknown age. We then eliminated those samples classified as low quality when they were in conjunction with at least two other consecutive samples of high quality on the same source. Next, samples collected opportunistically were removed if there were multiple samples collected from a single source. Due to the fact that multiple, consecutive samples collected at the same time from the same source tend to identify the same individual (for example, three tufts of hair taken from the barbed-wire on the same day; D. Paetkau, oral commun., Wildlife Genetics International, 2006), samples collected from a single source that contained ≥ 3 consecutive samples were removed in alternating fashion. The last selection criteria removed low quality samples from a single source where multiple (non-consecutive) samples were present. All selected hair samples were submitted to Dr. David Paetkau (Wildlife Genetics International, Nelson, BC, Canada) to be analyzed for bear species, sex, and individual identity using standard analytical procedures.

Remote Cameras and Analysis of Bear Activity Data

Sony® handheld cameras (DCR-TRV460 Sony Handycam®) were installed in all study sites (fig. 7). These cameras were selected because they contain a time-lapse recording option. Cameras were set to record a 0.5-second segment of video per minute, 24 hours per day (called a sequence during tape analysis). This setting permitted cameras to run continuously for 9.4 days before we had to reload a new video cassette. In this way, monitoring with the cameras represented instantaneous scan sampling procedures commonly used for recording behavioral data (Altmann, 1974). Each camera was connected to a 12-volt, 100-aH gel-cell battery and an 80-watt solar panel. For protection from curious bears, a portable electric fence was erected around each camera unit. Placement of camera units was dependent on the surrounding topography; however, high points were selected to maximize the amount of area that was monitored. Video cassettes were changed during each field visit.

As video cassettes were played back on a television, we were able to extract bear activity data. Each tape was reviewed twice to ensure accuracy. A total of 1,440 sequences (24 hours per day × 60 sequences per hour) were recorded daily. While observing these video tapes, each sequence was marked as having bears, humans, or both present or absent. After viewing, data were grouped by hour. Summed sequences of bears present in these hour groups were used for all subsequent analyses.

To calculate a metric for bear activity levels, the number of film sequences with bears present was divided by the total number of viewable sequences during a given hour. All independent bears (for example, those without dependent offspring) were individually counted, whereas females with dependent cubs were scored as a single bear, even though multiple bears were present. "Viewable sequences" were those that were not too dark or obscured (for example, by fog or sunlight direction on the lens). In this way, bear activity could be thought of as the percentage of the defined time period that bears were present. This also could be thought of as a surrogate for animal minutes, a metric used in many behavioral studies (Olson and Gilbert, 1994).

Bear Forage Diversity Index

During field visits, the presence, abundance, and phenology of key bear foods was recorded (data sheet, appendix 2). Phenology was assigned according to a list of phenological classifications presented in appendix 3. Potential forage items, based on experience and the literature, observed in the field were noted. Direct observation of foraging, or obvious signs of use, also were recorded opportunistically. To create a relative index of bear forage species for each site, the count of species present at a site was divided by the total number of species observed across all sites. This generated an index with a value that ranged from 0 to 1.0.

Ranking Study Sites by Degree of Use by Bears

Due to the relatively low levels of bear activity at sites we monitored, it was not possible to statistically evaluate inter-site differences. However, to rank sites relative to one another, we evaluated them by the following criteria: (1) average bear activity recorded on remote cameras, (2) areal extent of each site (km^2), (3) percent coverage of potential food species, (4) forage phenology, (5) number of scats encountered, (6) number of hair samples collected, and (7) number of individual bears identified by molecular genetic analysis. For each of these criteria, each site was ranked against all others, receiving a value of 1–8, 8 being the lowest value. For six variables (excluding area size ranking), rank was averaged, resulting in an overall ranking for each site.

Results

Habitat Mapping and Vegetation Analysis

Eight habitat types were identified in our eight study sites (table 2, appendix 1). Most habitat descriptions were consistent with types identified in Viereck and others (1992), but deviations were observed. The relatively recent de-glaciation of GLBA (< 200 years; Vequist, 1989) has resulted in sites dominated by ecotones rather than mature seral stages.

Generally, the habitat type closest to the waterline was the *halophytic wet forb/gramminoid herbaceous habitat*, typically dominated by species such as goose tongue (*Plantago maritima*), alkali grass (*Puccinellia nutkaensis*), arrow grass (*Triglochin maritimum*), and various sedges (*Carex* spp.; table 3a). This habitat type occurred in five of eight sites and represented an average percent cover of 21.8 ± 11.4 percent. Total bear forage coverage in this habitat was relatively high at 46.2 ± 8.9 percent, although, depending on the site, it represented a small percentage of total forage coverage for all sites combined (26.4 ± 28.5 percent). The exception to this occurred at the Wolf Point study site, where the halophytic zone occupied 38.2 percent of the study site and represented 76.2 percent of the total forage coverage (table 2).

The next habitat type frequently encountered in our study sites was *dry graminoid herbaceous habitat type*, dominated by food species such as rye grass (*Elymus arenarius*), goose tongue, and sedge, with small inclusions of forb communities (*Conioselium chinense, Fragaria chiloensis*, table 3b). This habitat was present in all study sites and composed 15.0 ± 6.2 percent of total cover. The overall coverage of potential bear forage species in this habitat type was relatively low at 21.6 ± 19.4 percent. The total bear forage species coverage for this habitat type across all study sites also was low at 7.3 ± 4.6 percent (table 2).

The *low open scrub habitat type*, located just upland from the dry graminoid herbaceous habitat, represented an average of 22.4 ± 18.6 percent of the study site. The coverage of potential bear food species in this zone was highly variable, ranging from 105.9 percent in highly vegetated study sites to 2.8 percent in early seral stage, sparse areas (average 47.3 ± 37.9 percent). Due to high variability within this habitat type, it is difficult to provide a generic description. The number of bear forage species occurring within this habitat type was highly variable across study sites. Several graminoid species (*Elymus arenarius*, *Carex* spp.), along with a large variety of forbs (*Oxytropis campestris*, *Hedysarum alpinum*, *Angelica* spp., *Conioselium chinense*, *Equisetum* spp.), and berry producing plants (*Shepherdia canadensis*, *Fragaria chiloensis*, *Rubus spectabilis*), varied greatly in percent coverage (table 3c). Bear food species found in the low open scrub habitat represented 22.3 ± 16.0 percent of the total food coverage in our study sites (table 2).

Several small areas representing distinct habitat types were present in a few study sites (*wet graminoid herbaceous, dry forb herbaceous*). Although they occasionally had high food coverages, these areas did not represent a significant proportion of habitat types in which they were found; they represented less than 3 percent of the study site and less than 2.5 percent of the total food coverage in those areas (table 2). Several important bear food species were found in these small habitats, including graminoid (*Carex* spp., *Elymus arenarius*) and forb species *Hedysarum alpinum*, *Fragaria chiloensis*, table 3d).

The *closed tall scrub habitat type*, occupying the final upland habitat in six of our eight study sites, represented 43.3 ± 16.9 percent of the study area (all eight sites combined). The extent inland that these habitats would be surveyed was pre-defined to end at a line 50 m inland from its beach-ward edge, which makes comparing it to other habitat types problematic. In the *low open scrub habitat*, food species and coverages were highly variable (table 2). Potential food species found in the tall closed scrub were similar to those that occurred in the low open scrub (tables 3c and 3e). Food species coverage ranged from 4.8 to 87.9 percent of this habitat type (average 46.2 ± 33.2 percent), and represented 8.5 to 88.5 percent of the total food coverage found in our study sites (average 53.9 ± 30.4 percent).

In two of eight study sites, upland areas were occupied by a *closed needle leaf forest* type (Tlingit Point, Sandy Cove). This habitat occupied an average of 61.4 percent of the total area in our study sites, although it is important to remember that the width of these habitats was pre-defined (50 m in from the edge of the habitat). Food coverage in this type was 29.8 percent, although the two study sites were quite different. Needle leaf forest at Tlingit Point was minimally represented, with food species coverage of 16.4 percent and containing only a small number of potential food species. In contrast, the forest in Sandy Cove was much more diverse, with food species coverage of 43.1 percent (table 2). Devils club (*Oplopanax horridus*) and salmonberry (*Rubus spectabilis*) were the most common food species found under the forest canopy (table 3f). A total of 52.2 percent of the total food coverage present in Sandy Cove and Tlingit Point was attributable to food species found in this habitat.

Bear Sign Assessment

Although all bear sign encountered was mapped and incorporated into GIS (fig. 8), not all bear sign could be easily quantified. For example, the length of bear trails often was indeterminate and trail age also was difficult to assess. Bear digs also were difficult to quantify as they were often extensive, obscuring individual digs.

The number of scats encountered during each site visit was readily quantified. Sandy Cove had the most scats ($n = 239$), followed by Russell Passage ($n = 163$), and Queen Inlet ($n = 116$; table 4). The remaining five sites had relatively low scat counts (all < 45). The number of hair samples collected in the Queen Inlet study site was the highest ($n = 225$), followed by Russell Passage ($n = 141$), and Reid Inlet ($n = 126$; table 4). Queen Inlet had the highest number of identified rub trees and chew logs, followed by Sandy Cove, Russell Passage, and Reid Inlet. Wolf Point had the highest number of bear beds, followed by Reid Inlet and Queen Inlet (table 4).

Based on a cursory analysis of the gross contents of scats encountered in our study sites, forb and graminoid species were the largest diet item for bears, particularly early in the season. The flowers, stems, and seeds of field oxytrope were a large component of scats in Queen Inlet and Russell Passage. Graminoid species such as rye grass and sedge commonly were found throughout the season for brown bears, and alkali grass also was commonly found in black bear scats. Horsetail (*Equisetum arvense*) also was found in scats collected from most study sites throughout the season. A thorough examination of scat contents would have yielded more information, but evidence from the field suggests that bears used many species of umbels (*Conioselium chinense, Heracleum lanatum, Angelica* spp.), as well as the roots of sweetvetch, vetch, groundcone (*Boschniakia rossica*), and field oxytrope. Berry use, as inferred by gross scat analysis, was high in GLBA, starting in June with the maturation of strawberry and salmonberry and continuing through July and into late August when devils club, soapberry (*Sherperdia canadensis*), bearberry (*Arctostaphylos uva-ursi*), and other species became prevalent.

Scat and hair collections both showed seasonal peaks (fig. 9). The number of hair samples collected was lowest in early June, peaked from late June through late July, and decreased again through the end of August. The number of scats observed was high through mid-June, decreased towards the end of June, and peaked again from late June through late July before decreasing through the end of August.

Number and Species of Bears Using the Sites

A total of 356 hair samples were collected in eight study sites in 2005 (table 5). Of these, 264 were selected and submitted for genetic analysis. The overall success rate for individual identification from our submitted samples was 54.17 percent. Samples collected at hair traps had the highest success rate at 63.8 percent, while samples collected opportunistically had the lowest at 22.2 percent (table 6).

A total of 47 individual bears were identified across all sites by molecular genetic analysis of hairs (table 7). Most bears identified were brown bears (*Ursus arctos,* 34 of 47), with a male to female sex ratio of 1.06:1.0. Thirteen black bears (*Ursus americanus*) were identified with a male to female ratio of 2.25:1.0. Black bears were identified at two sites, and Tlingit Point was the only site in which black and brown bears were identified. Queen Inlet had the highest number of bears identified with 13 brown bears, while only a single brown bear was identified at the Tarr Inlet site (table 7). Most bears were identified multiple times, at multiple sources, and/or on multiple collection trips (table 8).

Bear Activity Based on Remote Camera Data

Remote cameras in GLBA filled 76 video cassettes for a total of 682 camera days (table 9). The overall bear activity rate (a unit-less value representing a ratio of total number of minutes observed divided by total number of minutes filmed) for all sites combined was 0.014 ± 0.10 (table 10). This translates into bear presence from an average of 16 minutes per day up to a maximum of 131 minutes per day during visible daylight hours (assumed to be from 3:00 to 23:00). Queen Inlet had the highest recorded bear activity of 0.041 ± 0.18, and Tlingit Point had the lowest at 0.001 ± 0.01 (table 11; fig. 10). Activity peaks occurred early in the season in 2004 and 2005, while the secondary peak in 2005 occurred about 2 weeks later than in 2004. Average activity decreased to low levels towards the end of July through the end of August (fig. 15).

Bear Forage Diversity Index

By taking the total number of bear forages present at any given site and dividing that by the total number of bear forages present across all sites, a bear forage diversity index (BFDI) for each site was calculated. The site with the most diverse offering of bear forage was Sandy Cove (BFDI = 0.92), followed by the Russell Passage Site (BFDI = 0.81), then Tlinglit Point (BFDI = 0.76), Reid and Queen Inlets (both with BFDI = 0.68), Tarr Inlet (BFDI = 0.54), Wolf Point (BFDI = 0.49), and Johns Hopkins, the least diverse site (BFDI = 0.24).

Site Ranking by Bear Activity

Based on the site ranking procedure, the following areas are listed from least valuable to highest: Johns Hopkins, Tarr Inlet, Tlinglit Point, Wolf Point, Reid Inlet, Sandy Cove, Queen Inlet and Russell Passage (table 12; fig. 15). The Queen Inlet, Sandy Cove, and Russell Passage study sites consistently ranked highest for all variables of interest (for example, bear activity, areal extent, food coverage, bear sign, scat numbers, bear numbers, and forage phenology; table 12; fig. 15). Sites in Johns Hopkins and Tarr Inlets consistently ranked lowest with the exception of camera activity data.

Bear Movements

Although not a stated objective of this study, several bear movements between our study sites were identified through hair DNA analysis. A male brown bear identified from hair collected during the mid to late June sampling period in Queen Inlet also was identified in Russell Passage during the late June to mid-July time period. The Euclidian distance (that is, straight line) from the bear's location in Queen Inlet to its location in Russell Passage is about 16.6 km (10.4 mi). Modeling likely travel paths between the areas yields distances ranging from 18.6 to 61.2 km (11.6 and 38.0 mi, respectively; fig. 15). Hence, this bear traveled a minimum of 37.2 km (23.1 mi) while making a round trip excursion from Queen Inlet to Russell Passage.

Another male brown bear identified from hair collected in late June to mid-July in Tarr Inlet also was identified from hair collected in the mid- to late July period in Reid Inlet. Euclidian distance from the Tarr Inlet to Reid Inlet study site is 14.1 km (8.8 mi). The shortest coastal travel path between the two sites is 18.6 km (11.56 mi; fig. 14). This bear traveled a minimum of 58.0 km (34.8 mi) during the trip from Tarr Inlet to Reid Inlet.

Discussion

Remote Camera Data

Coastal areas of GLBA contain many important forage resources for bears, both in the early spring when other resources are less available, as well as later when berry crops mature and salmon enter streams. Flat coastal areas are the easiest way for bears to move around the bay. Remote camera data show relatively light use of areas monitored, suggesting that bears use other habitats extensively year round. It also is possible that bears choose to move around and forage in various productive areas, increasing their odds of discovering good food resources or potential mates. Bears foraging primarily on vegetation require anywhere from 8 to 12 hours of foraging time per day to sustain body weight, depending on the bears' mass (Rode and others, 2001; Smith and Partridge, 2004). Even given the maximum number of hours we documented bears using a given study site (the maximum was 4.4 hours), a bear still would have to continue foraging for another 4 hours simply to maintain body weight (Rode and others, 2001).

Bear activity recorded with remote camera units at GLBA was relatively low and highly variable within and between study sites. This made comparisons between seasons, time periods, and study sites problematic, limiting the evaluation of the camera activity data to the analysis of trends in activity. When bear activity is combined from all study sites, the temporal pattern was crepuscular with activity peaks early in the morning and evening. This observed pattern is typical of North American ursids, with the early morning peak lower than that in the evening (Smith, 2002; fig. 15). However, peaks and intensities of bear activity were not consistent between the 2 years of study (2004–05). Bear activity intensity over the course of the study, however, was fairly consistent between years as well as between study sites. Activity generally was relatively high in early to mid-June and then decreased towards the end of June. A secondary activity peak occurred from early to late July before decreasing to low levels towards the end of August. Activity patterns recorded with remote cameras generally were consistent with data from hair and scat collections. This pattern likely is a reflection of bear foraging being focused on early stages of plant phenological development. Hence, bears initially forage on newly emergent coastal vegetation, then move up in elevation as green-up progresses. When coastal berries mature, bears are drawn back to coastal areas. Following the peak of coastal berry availability, bear use decreases again as berry crops under the vegetation canopy mature and coastal vegetation becomes highly fibrous and poorly digestible. Additionally, salmon become available in certain areas, which likely causes bears to target this resource. Activity may have increased after we ceased monitoring sites as spawning salmon became available at the end of August. The temporal-spatial patterns of spawning salmon are poorly described for the western and eastern arms GLBA, but each of our study sites had some degree of spawners present, as observed anecdotally.

We experienced several problems with remote cameras. Mechanical failures aside, there were several problems with camera placement and effectiveness of this approach. One problem with this method of recording bear activity is that it cannot evaluate nocturnal bear activity. Several studies have found a primarily diurnal activity pattern for black and brown bears (Lariviere and others, 1994; MacHutchon and others, 1998), although there is evidence that activity can occur at night, particularly on salmon streams (Reimchen, 1998; Klinka and Reimchen, 2002). Cameras could not monitor bear activity within the closed tall scrub and closed needle leaf forest habitats, extensive units in most sites that contained relatively high food coverage. The largest problem with remote camera units was that the coverage area and view shed varied from site to site. Although there were a number of camera units that captured most of the study site in Queen Inlet, Sandy Cove, Tarr Inlet, and Johns Hopkins Inlet, the others could not be positioned as effectively. The Reid Inlet camera could not monitor the entire site, and based on evidence from bear scat locations, areas that were hidden may have contained the most bear activity. Wolf Point and Tlingit Point cameras, in addition to failing to work during the 2005 field season, were unable to monitor substantial areas. The Russell Passage camera also had several problems. The camera had to be placed on an island at a distance (> 400 m) from the study site and zoomed in, which generated a very shallow depth of field in the view. Additionally, fog and rain easily obscured the camera's view shed given its great distance to the site.

Even with some technical problems, remote video cameras units performed relatively well and were not visually intrusive to visitors. Although these cameras yielded useful information on bear presence in most of the study sites, this type of remote video monitoring may be best suited for use in a small area, such as a stretch of salmon stream, rub tree, or trail.

Vegetation, Habitat, and Diet Analysis

Data from habitat mapping, vegetation analysis, and tracking of phenology provides a detailed profile of a subset of potential bear forages across study sites. We originally had intended to track seasonal nutrient availability across study sites, but were unable to do so due to limitations in time and personnel. Although we did not have enough time and money to perform nutritional analyses for plants collected in our study sites, general statements concerning the nutritional profile of potential food species can be made. There is relatively little variation in the gross energy and crude protein content of most above ground vegetation, but other plant components change throughout the year and have a substantial effect on the overall nutritional value (Partridge and others, 2001). The overall nutritional value of a plant is a complex measure that depends on the size and phenology of the plant, the nutritional components of the species, and the specific plant part analyzed. Although most plants increase in size through the growing season, which can increase intake rates for animals, their fiber content also increases, which reduces digestibility and decreases the plants' overall nutritional value. Flowers generally are low in fiber and are highly digestible, and seeds are high in fiber but also high in digestible protein. The stems and stalks of plants generally are more digestible early in the season when less fiber is required to support the plant, and roots and tubers can be high in energy early in the season before energy stores are mobilized for growing and late in the season when energy is being stored for the next growing season.

Berry producing shrubs and plants can achieve high fruit densities and offer bears high intake rates, but due to the low protein level of most fruit species bears must continue to consume food items with high levels of digestible protein (Welch and others, 1997; Rode and Robbins, 2000). Berries that contain oils, such as devils club and elderberry, have high gross energy contents (Partridge and others, 2001). It is suspected that soapberry also may be higher in energy levels than most berries (Robbins and others, 2004).

Meat sources, such as ungulates, can be an important source of nutrition for bears (Mattson, 1997; Hilderbrand and others, 1999; Jacoby and others, 1999), and salmon are one of the most important factors determining the population density of bears in coastal Alaska (Hilderbrand and others, 1999). There is little information on salmon abundance and availability in GLBA, particularly in sites we selected for study. Due to the relatively recent deglaciation of

GLBA, many streams within the park have only recently been colonized by salmon. Bear use of intertidal resources, such as barnacles, mussels, and clams, also has been found in several coastal areas of Alaska (Smith and Partridge, 2004). Although larger bears may not be able to efficiently use these resources to gain weight, intertidal resources are available year round (at low tides) and can provide certain bear cohorts with a valuable protein source (Smith and Partridge, 2004). Other potential animal protein sources include insects such as bees, wasps, and ants. Where large insect colonies or nests exist, bears can achieve high intake rates (Noyce and others, 1997; White and others, 1998).

Although information obtained through scat analysis offers insight regarding the diet of GLBA bears, there are several serious shortcomings. Scat analysis can only detect partially digested diet items; therefore, highly digestible diet items such as meat and fungi are under-represented and poorly digested items such as graminoid species are over-represented (Hilderbrand and others, 1999). Although correction factors have been measured for some diet items (Hewitt and Robbins, 1996), the effect that a highly variable diet has on these correction factors is unknown, and a correction factor for meat is dependent on the percentage of hair and connective tissue ingested, something which could not be determined in the field.

Based on a cursory analysis of the gross contents of scats encountered in our study sites, forb and graminoid species were the largest diet item for bears, particularly early in the season. The flowers, stems, and seeds of field oxytrope were a large component of scats in Queen Inlet and Russell Passage. Graminoid species such as rye grass and sedge commonly were found throughout the season for brown bears, while alkali grass was found in black bear scats. Horsetail (*Equisetum arvense*) also was found in scats collected from most study sites throughout the season. A thorough examination of scat contents would have yielded more information, but evidence from the field suggests that bears used many species of umbels (*Conioselium chinense, Heracleum lanatum, Angelica* spp.), as well as the roots of sweetvetch, vetch, groundcone (*Boschniakia rossica*), and field oxytrope. Berry use, as inferred by gross scat analysis, was high in GLBA, starting in June with the maturation of strawberry and salmonberry and continuing through July and into late August when devils club, soapberry (*Sherperdia canadensis*), bearberry (*Arctostaphylos uva-ursi*), and other species became prevalent.

There was not much evidence of a dependence on terrestrial meat sources by GLBA bears, although scats were occasionally found with hair and connective tissue. One source of terrestrial food for bears in many of our study sites was wasps. In Sandy Cove, Wolf Point, and Russell Passage, the remains of several nests of paper wasps were found, along with wasp exoskeletons and nest material in scats. The use of barnacles (*Balanus spp.*) and mussels (*Mytilus edulis*) was common across study sites and seasons. Barnacle exoskeletons were more commonly observed in bear scats than mussels, although sympatric in intertidal areas. In late August 2005, salmon became common in scats from specific areas such as Wolf and Tlingit Points. Evaluation of salmon dependence was difficult because field work terminated just as salmon were entering streams.

A recent study of the stable carbon and nitrogen isotope signatures of hair samples collected in GLBA offers insight regarding the diet of GLBA coastal bears (Mowat and Heard, 2006). Mowat and Heard (2006) determined through analysis of brown bear guard hairs collected in GLBA that the proportion of assimilated carbon and nitrogen coming from marine sources was 31 percent. This is low when compared to other coastal bear populations (Hilderbrand and others, 1999; Mowat and Heard, 2006), but perhaps higher than expected based on field observations made during this study. Marine carbon and nitrogen is assumed to have come from salmon, although bears obviously use other marine sources (for example, barnacles, mussels, and rock gunnels). There are large enough differences in the isotopic signatures of intertidal animals and salmon to discriminate dietary proportions of each based on sulfur isotopes, so it is important to evaluate potential intertidal use as it contributes to the overall percentage of marine derived nutrients (K. Rode, written commun., US Fish and Wildlife Service, 2006). Importantly, the 31 percent value represents the assimilated carbon and nitrogen coming from marine sources and does not indicate the total biomass consumed. Thus, based on the analysis of isotopic analyses, marine protein sources are an important part of the yearly diet of bears in GLBA, but vegetation likely composes most of the biomass consumed by bears. The Mowat and Heard (2006) study was broad in scope and a low number of hair samples were used in the calculation for GLBA bears. Due to differences in salmon run strength, species, and timing, additional isotope work would help shed light on the dynamics of coastal bear salmon use in GLBA. It also would be useful to determine which bear cohorts use salmon and to what extent, as females with dependent young may forgo salmon use to avoid intra-specific predation on the young (Ben-David and others, 2004).

Habitat

Low open scrub habitat was the most diverse vegetation community type among study sites. Areas of low open scrub had high forage coverage and diversity and also were areas of high bear activity. This habitat type had numerous forb and graminoid species as well as berry-producing plants. Heavily foraged species in this habitat type were field oxytrope, sweetvetch (*Hedysarum alpinum*), strawberry, soapberry (*Shepherdia canadensis*), and several species of umbels (*Heracleum lanatum, Angelica* spp., *Conioselium chinense).*

Dry graminoid herbaceous and halophytic wet graminoid herbaceous types had the lowest species diversity and bear forage coverage. Other habitat types such as wet graminoid herbaceous and dry forb herbaceous, although they had potential forage species, represented a small fraction of the overall study site and consequently contributed only slightly to the study site's overall food coverage.

Upland habitat types, closed tall scrub, and closed needle leaf forest represented a large percentage of study sites and contributed substantially to overall food coverages. Bear forages in these habitats were chiefly berry producing plants, such as soapberry and strawberry in the closed tall scrub habitats, and devils club and salmon berry in the closed needle leaf forest. These foods matured later in the season and likely accounted for the corresponding depression of bear activity within beach areas.

Bear Sign Assessment

Mapping of bear sign provided a measure of bear use within study sites. It was difficult, however, to accurately measure some signs including the beginning and end of indistinct trails, indiscrete bear beds, faint tracks, and delineation of individual digs within well excavated areas. The most useful quantitative measure of bear activity was scats. Hair also was a good quantitative measure, although occasionally it was difficult to discriminate individual samples. Bear activity, as inferred by scat frequency, follows the same seasonal pattern documented with remote cameras: activity was relatively high in May, decreased significantly by the end of June, and then peaked again by the end of July, before decreasing into August.

Bear activity patterns based on hair captures did not follow camera-based activity patterns as closely as scat data. Hair-based activity patterns occurred at the same time as those seen on camera tape, but hair capture rates were low in the early parts of June. A male bias for bear use of rub trees and scented hair traps has been reported (Kendall and McKelvey, 2008). Additionally, rubbing behavior is a means of communication and can involve complex bear behavioral characteristics that may change over the course of the year (Green and Mattson, 2003).

Hair Collection and DNA Analysis

A large number of hair samples were collected in both years of study (2004–05; $n = 883$). Due to budget shortfalls, we were able to analyze only a fraction of hair samples collected ($n = 264$). We restricted analysis to samples collected in 2005. Inexplicably, the percentage of successful identifications (54 percent) was low when compared to similar studies. It is possible that DNA in hair samples degraded before returning from the field, although samples that had been unpreserved for 2 weeks have yielded good results (D. Paetkau, written commun., Wildlife Genetics International, 2006). We oven-dried hair samples and stored them with silica desiccant to remove residual moisture, so it seems unlikely that the storage method damaged hair follicles.

Forty-seven individual bears were identified from hair collected in 2005. Although they generally occupied different ecological niches, areas with black bears were not considered separately from brown bear areas, primarily due to the fact that only two sites contained black bears. Generally, bears were identified from multiple hair samples, often collected on multiple sources, and on separate collection trips. We identified new individuals throughout the season, suggesting that we were not able to adequately capture all bears in our study sites. Alternately, GLBA bears may have little seasonal range fidelity, traveling widely throughout their home range.

Rub trees, whether enhanced with barbed wire or not, were excellent places to collect hair samples, although hair capture success rates were similar to other hair capture methods (for example, barbed wire traps). Some tree species, such as spruce (*Picea sitchensis*), were better at holding large samples of hair than others (for example, alder or cottonwood). However, some study sites lacked rub trees, resulting in fewer hair samples. Similarly, chew logs proved to be a good source for hair collection, particularly if preserved with creosote. Logs that have been soaked in creosote for preservation attract bears which rub there and the splintered wood catches hairs in the process. Opportunistically collected samples (that is, from tree branches over-hanging trails or ground rubbing sites) had the lowest success rates of all hair collection methods, likely due to the indeterminate age of the samples.

The performance of scented hair traps was poor, even though they achieved the highest hair capture success rate. Several factors contributed to the lower than expected success of scented hair traps. First, we were unable to adequately "age" the scent attractant, meaning that the scent was not nearly as strong as it could have been. We did, however, age the scent solution for 2 weeks prior to each field trip, but it quickly lost its odor when applied in the field. A weak scent in conjunction with a prevalent on-shore breeze likely resulted in a greatly reduced ability to attract bears. Secondly, it was sometimes difficult to find an appropriate location for the scent trap, as sites had to be visually obscured from visitors and at a safe distance from likely camping sites to minimize the likelihood of bear/human interactions. Only one bear (black bear) visited a trap site twice. This observation is consistent with work by M.L. Gibeau (biologist, Parks Canada, oral. commun. 2006) that showed that only 40 percent of brown bears that encountered scent traps did not enter them. Therefore, care should be exercised when using hair traps to answer specific questions such as the size and trend of bear populations, as well as evaluating site fidelity.

Bear Movements

Two instances of bears visiting multiple study sites were identified through DNA analysis. Both bears were males, and males typically have larger home ranges and move more than females, particularly during the breeding season as they search for potential mates (Dahle and others, 2006). Young male bears have been implicated in a substantial proportion of bear/human interaction at GLBA (T. Smith, unpub. data, 2006), so in cases where bear interactions have occurred, it may be ineffective to close a small geographic area surrounding the conflict site. A much larger sample size of bear movements is needed to better understand bear movements and their impact on area closures. Given the time commitment, cost, and difficulties associated with bear hair collection and DNA analysis, other methods for determining bear movements (for example, conventional radio-tagging and telemetry) may prove more effective if such data are deemed important for management decisions.

Site Ranking by Bear Activity

Ranking of study site variables provided a useful means of evaluating differences in bear use among the study sites. Sites in Queen Inlet, Russell Passage, and Sandy Cove consistently ranked at the top in bear use and habitat quality and our field observations support them. These also are known locally as high use bear areas. There was a suite of potentially important variables we could not address, such as the availability of alternative foraging areas and travel corridors, which clearly play a role in bear use of an area. Nonetheless, this ranking should provide biologists a benchmark for comparison against which future management decisions can be based.

Closure Areas Evaluations

An objective of this project was to evaluate sites in Tarr and Johns Hopkins Inlets and Sandy Cove that have been closed to camping for the past decade. The average ranking of these sites was 6.2, 6.8, and 2.3, respectively, based on a scale of 1–8, with 8 being the least important (table 12). Both Tarr and Johns Hopkins Inlets ranked third and fourth, respectively, in bear activity rates based on camera data, but no other measures indicated equivalent high use by bears. However, camera-based activity rankings lower than these (Russell Passage, Wolf Point, Tlingit Point, and Reid Inlet) had poor study site coverage and/or mechanical problems. Other bear activity measures taken at those sites indicate that bear activity was higher than the video record indicated. Potential bear habitat at both closure sites was relatively limited and did not contain a high diversity or quantity of potential bear food items. Bears were never observed in Tarr Inlet or Johns Hopkins Inlet by the field crews, although tracks and camera data did indicate use. It is possible that bears move through these areas and spend little time foraging and consequently leave little sign. We suspect that the relatively low amount of bear activity in these areas likely is due to the marginal habitats present. One salmon was seen in Tarr Inlet in entering a stream channel in the study site, but it is unknown if salmon successfully spawn there. The fact that a large group of sea birds (for example, gulls, terns, plovers, sandpipers, and oystercatchers) nest on beaches in the Johns Hopkins Inlet study site indicates that bears rarely visit the site.

The Sandy Cove study site, in comparison to the other closure areas, ranked highest in all measured variables. Only black bears were identified at Sandy Cove, although a salmon run in Spokane Cove just south of the study site may attract brown bears from up bay late in the season. Berry-producing species, dominant under the forest canopy, mature late in the season due to a lack of sunlight. Low open scrub habitat, while very diverse, was sparse and contributed only 12.2 percent of total food coverage at the site, and the closed needle leaf forest contributed 55.4 percent. In the two sites that consistently ranked high for brown bear activity, Russell Passage and Queen Inlet, low open scrub habitat represented both a larger portion of the study site as well as the total food coverage. Field oxytrope, soapberry, and sweet vetch, major constituents of brown bear scats we collected at the other study sites, were not found in scats from Sandy Cove. Black bears commonly were encountered at Sandy Cove, including sows with cubs of the year, and camera data indicated that bears forage extensively in the halophytic zone and the low open scrub habitat. The average rank value of this site was 2.33 (table 12), and no bear activity variable ranked lower than 4th. Whether bear activity here is high due to high quality habitat, a lack of substantial human activity, or some combination, is unknown. We did not monitor many sites south of Tlingit Point, and black bear activity in sites such as Geike Inlet or the Beardslee Islands may be comparable or greater than that documented in Sandy Cove. Regardless, based on all our measured indexes, there was substantial bear activity in Sandy Cove, although activity decreased sharply from the end of July through the end of August.

Bear Activity Assessment Techniques Summary

For clarity, we provide this summary of techniques used to assess levels of bear activity across study sites in GLBA.

Remote Camera Monitoring

Strengths: Remote cameras eliminate the need for observers to watch areas to record bear activity. These systems operate continuously and provide excellent insight regarding the diel patterns of bears in a given area. Additionally, precise time of day is recorded. Bear activity patterns in response to variables of interest (for example, human activity and weather), can be rigorously analyzed. Ultimately, they are cheaper and less invasive to have on site than human observers.

Weaknesses: Some visitors to wilderness areas object to having their presence and activity recorded by remote cameras. Additionally, to some persons, the mere presence of video camera systems degrades the quality of wilderness. Biologists using these camera systems must report data as "total bear minutes/hour" or use a similar index because individual bears cannot be identified within the view shed. Camera system placement is logistically difficult: gel-cell batteries (35 kg each) are burdensome to haul over rugged terrain; solar panels are large and bulky; excellent vantage points are rare or non-existent. Field personnel using and maintaining video systems must have a rudimentary understanding of electronics and be able to troubleshoot problems in the field. These systems have to be revisited on bi-weekly intervals for video-tape exchange. Video camera systems have to be within weather-proof housing and these were sometimes prone to moisture penetration resulting in camera failures. Additionally, camera systems have to be protected from curious bears with electric fencing, yet more equipment to deploy and another system that can fail. Image quality is affected by inclement weather (for example, heavy rain and fog) and the sun's glare on lenses. No data are collected in the night-time hours. Equipment malfunctions occurred frequently enough to be troubling: insufficient power resulting from low solar input, wire connection failures, moisture penetration into the camera house and wiring. Video-tape analysis is tedious and time consuming.

Summary: Video camera systems collect data continuously without the presence of human observers. These systems provide an index of bear activity based on direct observation of animals. They can verify presence/absence, time of day, activity patterns, and the response of bears to human activity, all useful information for park managers. However, in the rugged and remote wilderness of GLBA, deployment of these systems is problematic and the costs and benefits must be carefully considered in order to determine their applicability.

Bear Sign Indexes

Strengths: Site surveys resulting in tallies of bear sign (scat, rub trees, mark trails, forage utilization) are inexpensive and relatively easy to perform. Count data provides an index of bear activity relative to season as well as other sites.

Weaknesses: Without validation through direct observation, it is difficult to relate bear sign to actual levels of bear activity. This approach requires repeated visits to sites of interest on time scales appropriate for management questions. Although relatively minor, bear sign surveys can displace bears, trample vegetation, and degrade the wilderness quality of the area. It also is possible that not all bears leave discernible sign when passing through an area. More research is needed to increase our understanding of the correlation between bear sign and actual bear activity.

Summary: Bear sign counts are widely used in North America and are favored, in part, for their noninvasive nature. However, field crews conducting repeated surveys in wilderness are not noninvasive because bears are displaced and vegetation trampled. The strength of correlation of bear sign to bear activity is not well understood and needs to be further investigated before ascribing activity levels to areas based solely on sign surveys.

Site Vegetation Sampling

Strengths: Using the Daubenmire approach, or other vegetation sampling method, researchers are able to generate a relatively accurate description of a study site's vegetation community and determine the presence of bear forages. Such approaches have been widely used to relatively rank sites' values to bears based solely on their presumed forage value. These methods are time consuming but straightforward in application.

Weaknesses: Sampling is very time intensive, requires personnel skilled in plant identification, and can be difficult in densely vegetated scrub communities (for example, alder scrub). Without validation of the dependence of bears on various plant species within the GLBA area, the strength of the linkage between site forage and bear activity is questionable. Additionally, a site may have abundant forage but its physical proximity to other components of bear habitat certainly affects the degree of usage it receives. For example, a site may have abundant bear forage species but if bordered on either side by sheer cliffs it is not likely to receive much bear activity. The presence of salmon in late summer also can greatly influence a site's usage by bears and this has nothing to do with its bear forage suitability.

Summary: Vegetation sampling provides a fairly accurate depiction of vegetation community composition and is always a part of bear/habitat relationship studies. However, the linkages between bears and a given community are the result of a suite of variables including proximity to other forage resources, accessibility, and levels of human activity. The use of remotely sensed imagery (that is, satellite imagery) may circumvent the tedious nature of site sampling but issues of resolution must be addressed.

DNA Analysis

Strengths: This is a relatively noninvasive procedure allowing the identification of specific individuals and even genetic lineages. One never has to interact with bears directly to get hair samples for analysis and can get an idea of the number of bears present in a given area.

Weaknesses: DNA analysis requires the use of an attractive bait and hair collection substrate (for example, barbed wire and nails in carpet), which is seen by some as degrading to the wilderness qualities of GLBA. Additionally, visitors have expressed concerns over being in areas that contain bait/scent attractants, worrying that bear/human encounter rates may increase as a result. To conduct a scientifically rigorous study using this approach is quite expensive ($50/sample with hundreds to thousands of samples needed). Even with efficient hair collection methodology, DNA extraction rates can run low (as in this study), thereby decreasing the cost/benefit ratio. Some bears avoid hair snare apparatuses so this method may never be able to accurately depict the actual numbers of bears present in an area.

Summary: DNA analysis has been successful in areas (for example, Glacier National Park) where enough funding was provided to collect and analyze an appropriate number of samples. In the case of Glacier National Park, approximately $5 million in congressionally appointed funding was needed to use the DNA approach for population estimation. Although often described as a 'noninvasive' technique, this technique involves the construction of hair snaring barbed wire enclosures, deployment of scent-baits, and frequent trips by research personnel to the hair snaring site. Within parks and other protected areas, visitors may express frustration after encountering a hair-snaring station. This methodology is relatively noninvasive, compared to bear capture and handling in order to retrieve tissues for DNA extraction and analysis.

Conclusions

This study provides insight regarding the nature and intensity of bear activity at selected coastal sites within GLBA. We were able to construct a better understanding of bear/habitat relationships within GLBA by analyzing data collected with remote cameras, vegetation mapping and collections, and genetic analysis of bear hair. Although we do not know actual levels of bear activity at study sites, agreement among measures of bear activity (for example, sign counts, DNA analysis, and video record) lends support to our bear habitat assessments. Our work suggests that habitat evaluation, bear sign mapping, and periodic scat counts provide a useful index of bear activity for sites of interest.

GLBA is a dynamic and continually changing ecosystem, and these changes will influence bear habitat quality over time. Models predicting the pattern and timing of plant and animal succession in GLBA may help predict future patterns of bear use but much more information regarding regional bear forage resources is needed. Clearly, the ongoing establishment, persistence and health of anadromous fish populations will influence coastal bear populations in the future.

The relationship between bear numbers and likelihood of a negative bear/human interaction is complex and at times may have little to do with measurable site variables. Human group size, activity, and response to bears all influence the outcome of encounters. The disposition of individual bears, as well as their previous experience with humans, similarly can affect encounter outcome. Nonetheless, measuring bear numbers and activity in a specific site is a valid way to assess the risks of negative bear/human interactions because the more bears and people interact the more likely it is that a negative interaction will result.

GLBA resource managers must carefully determine information needs in order to prioritize future bear research. Questions regarding the size and structure of bear populations within the park are compelling but can be difficult to answer and the methods expensive and intrusive to the animals. Nevertheless, while this research project is typical of a noninvasive approach, it is important to recognize that researcher activity was present in potential bear habitat for several hours every 2 weeks, which in some study sites constituted the most human activity recorded at the site (GLBA, unpub. data, 2002). Additionally, an unnatural attractant also was used to increase the chance of obtaining bear hair, and camera equipment, barbed-wire, and fence posts were used in our study sites. Although sometimes it is unclear what constitutes real disturbance to animals, it is important to evaluate the potential costs of each research approach and weigh them against the potential benefit to the animals and the park resource personnel who manage them.

Acknowledgments

The authors would like to thank the following individuals who contributed greatly to this project: Drs. Scott Gende and Terry DeBruyn, and Jim Wilder for reviewing previous drafts. We're very grateful to the USGS and NPS for supporting the work. Karen Oakley of the USGS Alaska Science Center provided valuable insight regarding this manuscript. Additionally, we thank Nat Drumheller, Jessica Speed, Justin Smith, Monica Rectenwald, Phoebe Vanselow, Allison Banks, Susan Boudreau, and Rusty Yerxa.

References Cited

Altmann, J., 1974, Observational study of behavior—sampling methods: Behavior, v. 49, p. 227-267.

Ben-David, M., Titus, K., and Beier, L.R., 2004, Consumption of salmon by Alaskan brown bears—a trade-off between nutritional requirements and the risk of infanticide: Oecologia, v. 138, p. 465-474.

Dahle, B., Støenb, O., Swenson, J.E., 2006, Factors influencing home-range size in subadult brown bears: Journal of Mammalogy, v. 87, no. 5, p. 859-865.

Daubenmire, R., 1959, A canopy-coverage method of vegetational analysis: Northwest Science, v. 33, no. 1, p. 43-64.

Gilbert, B.K., and Lanner, R.M., 1995, Energy, diet selection and restoration of brown bear populations: Ursus, v. 9, p. 231-240.

Green, G.I., and Mattson, D.J., 2003, Tree rubbing by Yellowstone grizzly bears *Ursus arctos*: Wildlife Biology, v. 9, p. 1-9.

Hamilton, A.N., and Bunnell, F.L., 1987, Foraging strategies of coastal grizzly bears in the Kimsquit River Valley, British Columbia: Ursus, v. 7, p. 187-197.

Herrero, S., 2002, Bear attacks-their causes and avoidance, 2nd ed.: Piscataway, N.J., Winchester Press.

Hewitt, D.G., and Robbins, C.T., 1996, Estimating grizzly bear food habits from fecal analysis: Wildlife Society Bulletin v. 24, p. 547-550.

Hilderbrand, G.V., Schwartz, C.C., Robbins, C.T., Jacoby, M.E., Hanley, T.A., Arthur, S.M., and Servheen, C., 1999, The importance of meat, particularly salmon, to the body size, population productivity, and conservation of North American brown bears: Canadian Journal of Zoology, v. 77, p. 132-138.

Holm, G.W., Lindzey, F.G., and Moody, D.S., 1999, Interactions of sympatric black and grizzly bears in northwest Wyoming: Ursus, v. 11, p. 99-108.

Jacoby, M.E., Hilderbrand, G.V., Servheen, C., Schwartz, C.C., Arthur, S.M., Hanley, T.A., Robbins, C.T., and Michener, R., 1999, Trophic relations of brown and black bears in several western North American ecosystems: Journal of Wildlife Management, v. 63, no. 3, p. 921-929.

Kendall, K.C., and McKelvey, K.S., 2008, Hair Collection, *in* Long, R., MacKay, P., Ray, J., and Zielinski, W., eds., Noninvasive survey methods for North American Carnivores: Washington, DC, Island Press.

Klinka, D.R., and Reimchen, T.E., 2002, Nocturnal and diurnal foraging behavior of brown bears (*Ursus arctos*) on a salmon stream in coastal British Columbia: Canadian Journal of Zoology v. 80, p. 1317-1322.

Lariviere, S., Huot, J., and Samson, C., 1994, Daily activity patterns of female black bears in a northern mixed-forest environment: Journal of Mammalogy, v. 75, p. 613-620.

Lewis, T.M., Smith, T.S., Partridge, S.T., and Yerxa, R., 2006, Bear research and adaptive bear management in Glacier Bay National Park and Preserve—Poster presentation: Anchorage, AK, Wildlife Society 13th Annual Conference.

Mace, R.D., Manley, T.L., and Aune, K.E., 1994, Estimating grizzly bear population size using camera resightings: Wildlife Society Bulletin, v. 22, p. 74-83.

MacHutchon, A.G., Himmer, S., Davis, H., and Gallagher, M., 1998, Temporal and spatial activity patterns among coastal bear populations: Ursus, v. 10, p. 539-546.

MacHutchon, A.G., and Wellwood, D.W., 2003, Assessing the risk of bear-human interaction at river campsites: Ursus, v. 13, no. 14, p. 225-235.

Mattson, D.J., 1997, Use of ungulates by Yellowstone grizzly bears: Biological Conservation, v. 81, p. 161-177.

Mowat, G., and Heard, D.C., 2006, Major components of grizzly bear diet across North America: Canadian Journal of Zoology, v. 84, p. 473-489.

Noyce, K.V., Kannowski, P.B., and Riggs, M.R., 1997, Black bears as ant-eaters—seasonal associations between bear myrmecophagy and any ecology in north-central Minnesota: Canadian Journal of Zoology, v. 75, p. 1671-1686.

Olson, T.L., and Gilbert, B.K., 1994, Variable impacts of people on brown bear use of an Alaska river: Ursus, v. 9, p. 97-106.

Partridge, S.T., Nolte, D.L., Ziegltrum, G.J., and Robbins, C.T., 2001, Impacts of supplemental feeding on the nutritional ecology of black bears: Journal of Wildlife Management, v. 65, p. 191-199.

Reimchen, T.E., Nocturnal foraging behavior of black bear (*Ursus americanus*) on Moresby Island, British Columbia: Canadian Field Naturalist, v. 112, p. 446-450.

Robbins, C.T., Schwartz, C.C., and Felicetti, L.A., 2004, Nutritional ecology of ursids—a review of newer methods and management implications: Ursus, v. 15, p. 161-171.

Rode, K.D., and Robbins, C.T., 2000, Why bears consume mixed diets during fruit abundance: Canadian Journal of Zoology, v. 78, p. 1640-1645.

Rode, K.D., and Robbins, C.T., and Shipley, L.A., 2001, Constraints on herbivory by grizzly bears: Oecologia, v. 128, p. 62-71.

Samson, C., and Huot, J., 1995, Reproductive biology of female black bears in relation to body mass in early winter: Journal of Mammalogy, v. 76, p. 68-77.

Smith, T.S., 2002, Effects of human activity on brown bear use of the Kulik River, Alaska: Ursus, v. 13, p. 257-267.

Smith, T.S., and Partridge, S., 2004, Dynamics of intertidal foraging by coastal brown bears in southwestern Alaska: Journal of Wildlife Management, v. 68, no. 2, p. 233-240.

Vequist, G.W., 1989, Management of beach camping to reduce human-bear conflicts in Glacier Bay, Alaska: National Park Service – Glacier Bay National Park, 6 p.

Viereck, L.A., Dyrness, C.T., Batten, A.R., and Wenzlick, K.J., 1992, The Alaska vegetation classification: USDA Forest Service General Technical Report PNW-GTR-286.

Waits, L.P., and Paetkau, D., 2005, Noninvasive genetic sampling tools for wildlife biologists—a review of applications and recommendations for accurate data collection: Journal of Wildlife Management, v. 69, no. 4, p. 1419-1433.

Waits, L.P., Luikart, G., and Taberlet, P., 2001, Estimating the probability of identity among genotypes—Cautions and Guidelines: Molecular Ecology, v. 10, p. 249-256.

Welch, C.A, Keay, J., Kendall, K.C., and Robbins, C.T., 1997, Constraints on frugivory by bears: Ecology, v. 78, p. 1105-1119.

White, D. Jr., Kendall, C.K., and Picton, H.D., 1998, Grizzly bear feeding activity at alpine army cutworm moth aggregation sites in northwest Montana: Canadian Journal of Zoology, v. 76, 221-227.

Wielgus, R.B., and Bunnell, F.L., 1994, Sexual segregation and female grizzly bear avoidance of males: Journal of Wildlife Management, v. 58, p. 405-413.

Wielgus, R.B., and Bunnell, F.L., 2000, Possible negative effects of adult male mortality on female grizzly bear reproduction: Biological Conservation, v. 93, p. 145-154.

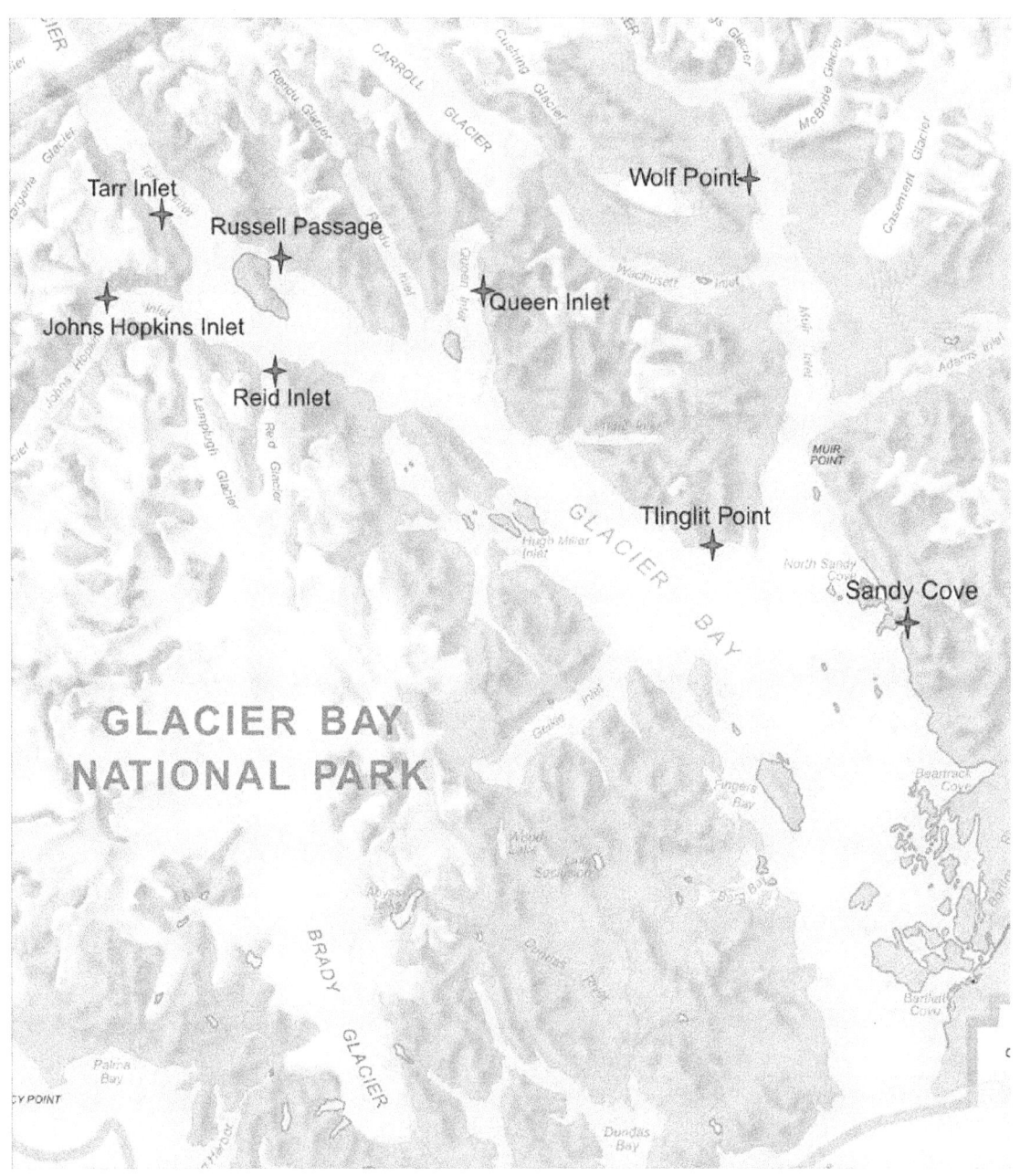

Figure 1. Location and names of selected study sites within Glacier Bay National Park and Preserve, Alaska (red stars).

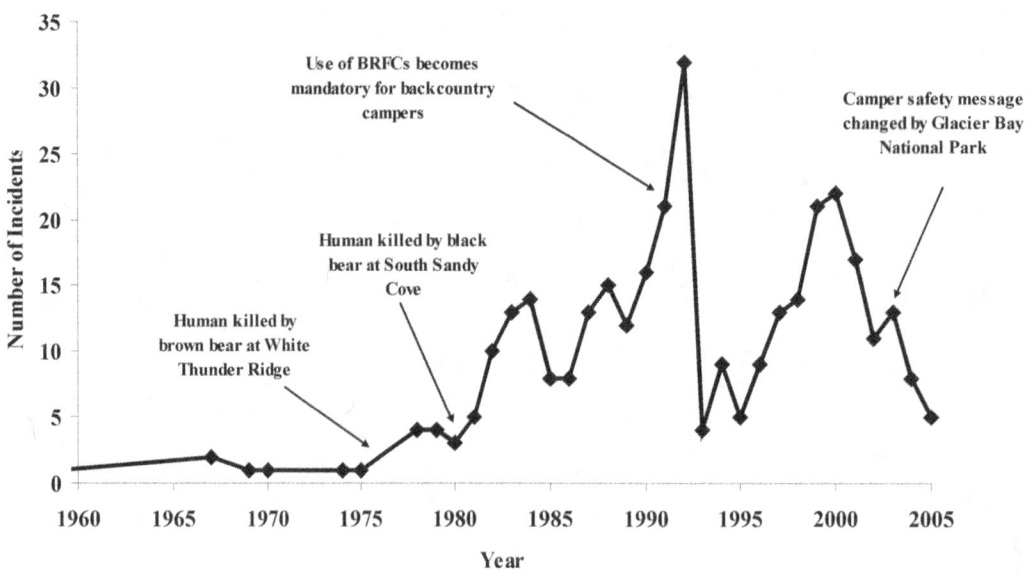

Figure 2. Number of bear-human incidents by year in GLBA, Alaska. Incidents are defined as bear-human encounters in which the bear behaved aggressively, made physical contact, obtained human food, and/or caused property damage.

Figure 3. Daubenmire plot (2 X 5 dm).

Rub Tree   Chew Log

Mark Trail   Bear Bed

Figure 4. Bear sign mapped in study sites.

Figure 5. Scented hair trap station, Sandy Cove, GLBA.

Figure 6. Barbed rub tree, Queen Inlet, GLBA

Figure 7. Remote camera unit, Reid Inlet, GLBA.

Figure 8. Example of bear sign maps.

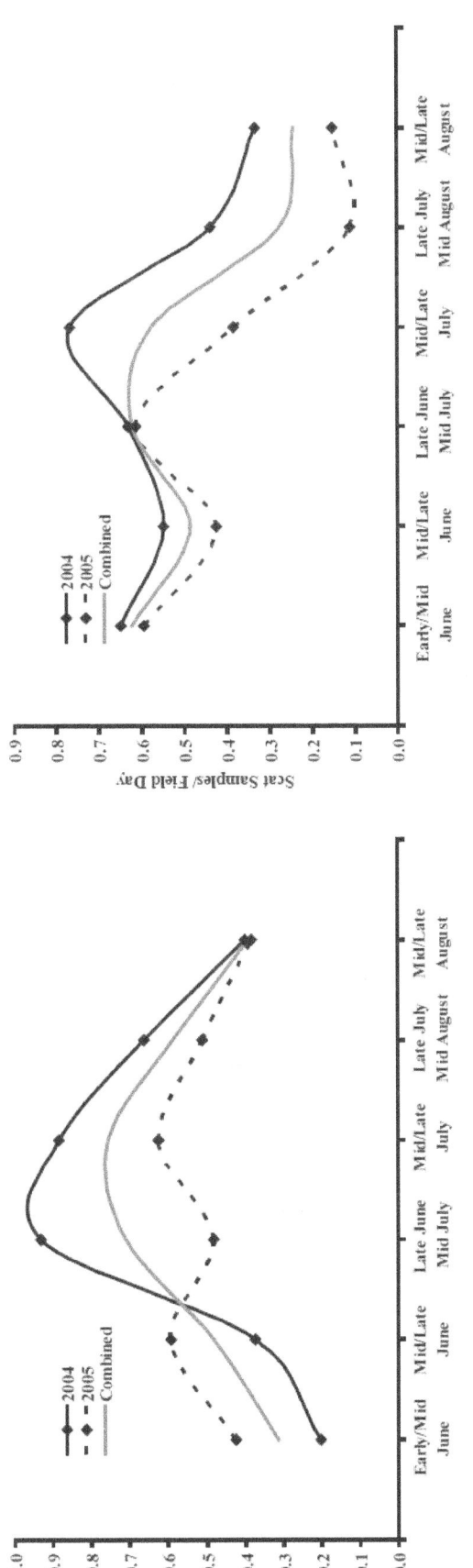

Figure 9. Seasonal collection patterns for hair and scat samples.

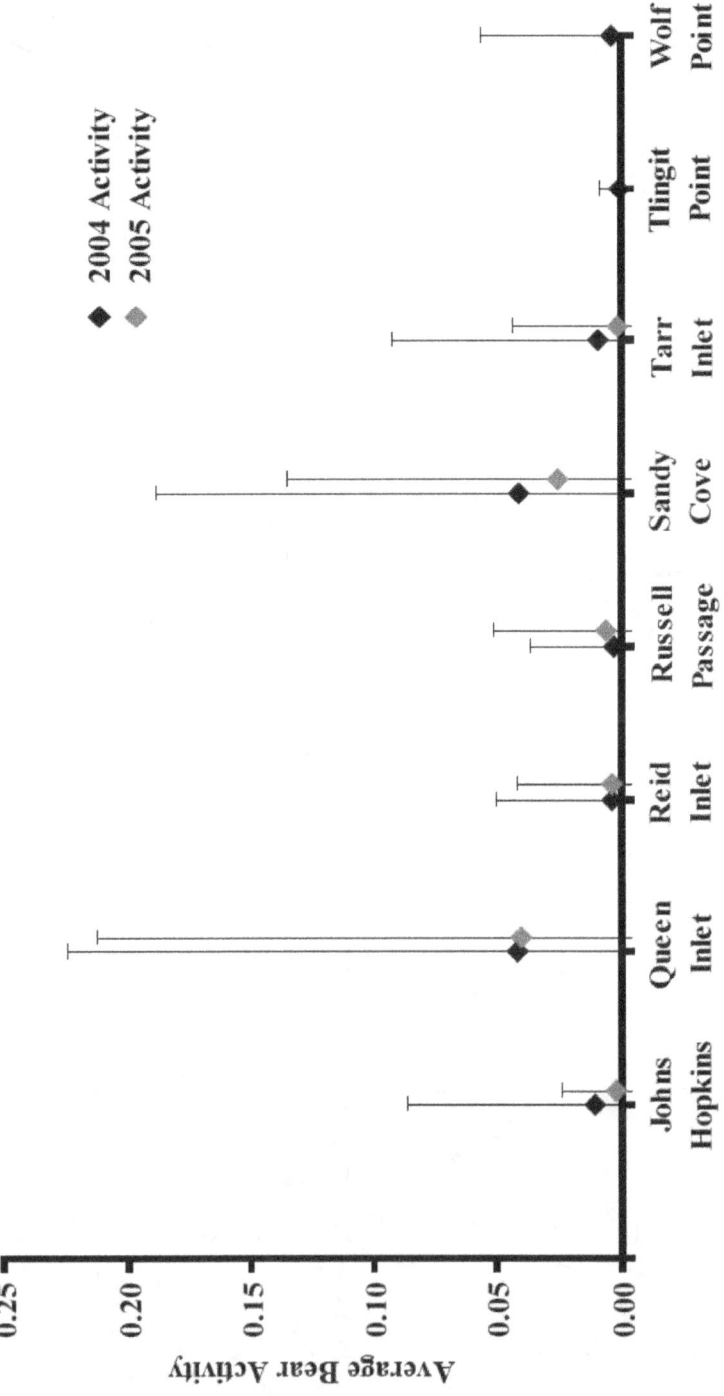

Figure 10. Bear activity rates from remote cameras for eight coastal study sites, GLBA.

34

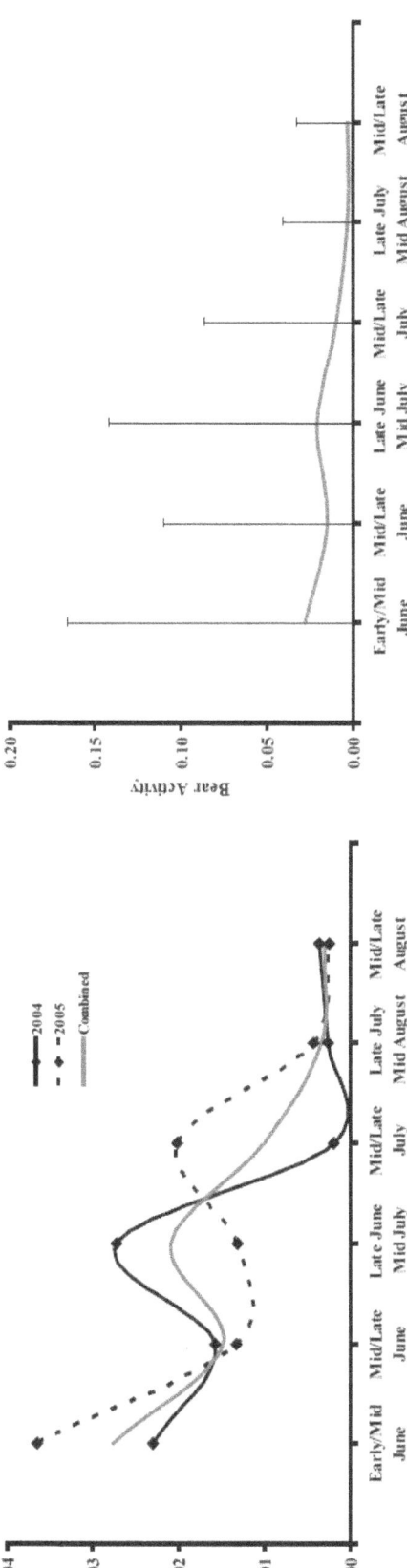

Figure 11. Bear activity rate by time of year.

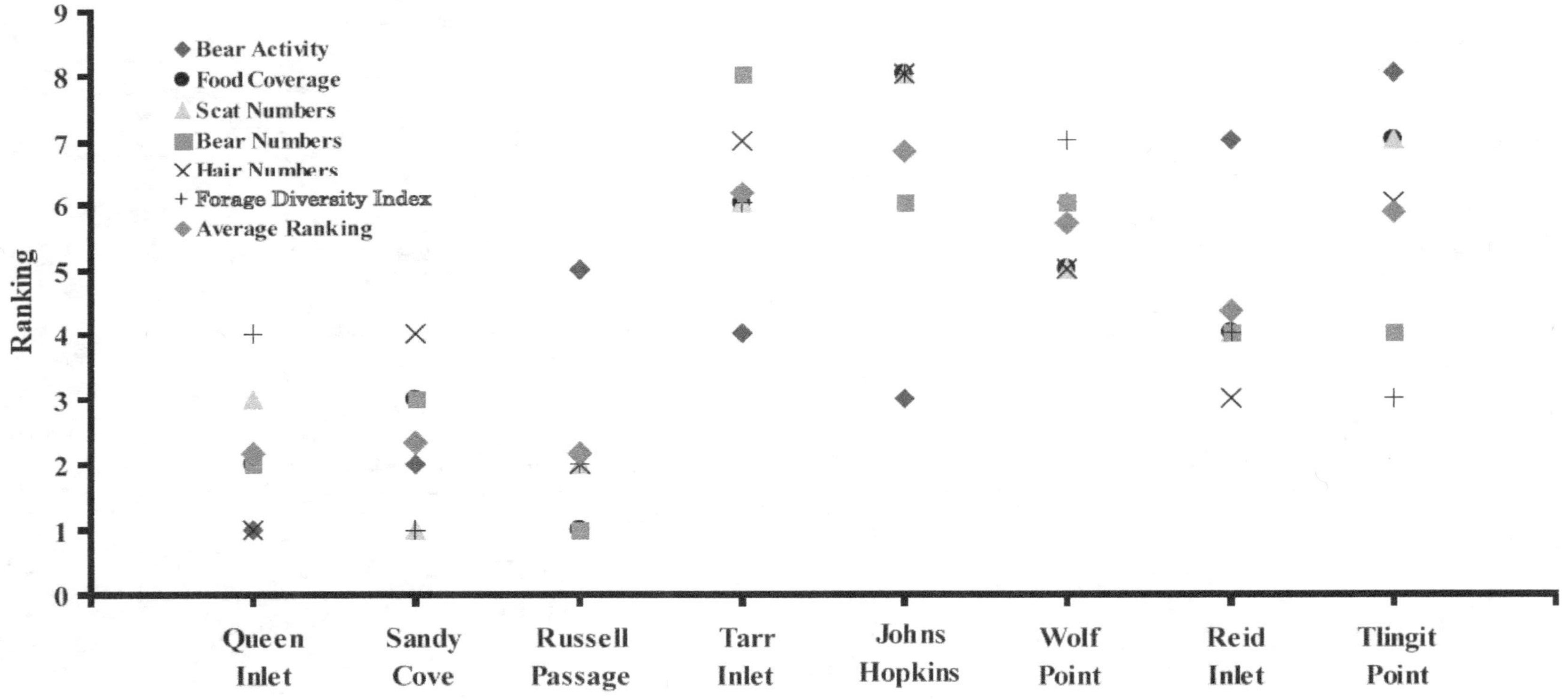

Figure 12. Study site rankings.

Figure 13. Graphic depicting a male grizzly bear's movements between the Queen Inlet and Russell Passage study sites. The blue represents the straight line distance (16.8 km), the red line represents a likely possible travel path (18.6 km), and the green line represents the longest coastal route (61.2 km).

37

Figure 14. Graphic depicting a male grizzly bear's movements between the Tarr Inlet and Reid Inlet study sites. The blue represents the straight line distance (14.1 km) and the red line represents a likely possible travel path (18.6 km), and the green line represents the longest coastal route (58.0 km).

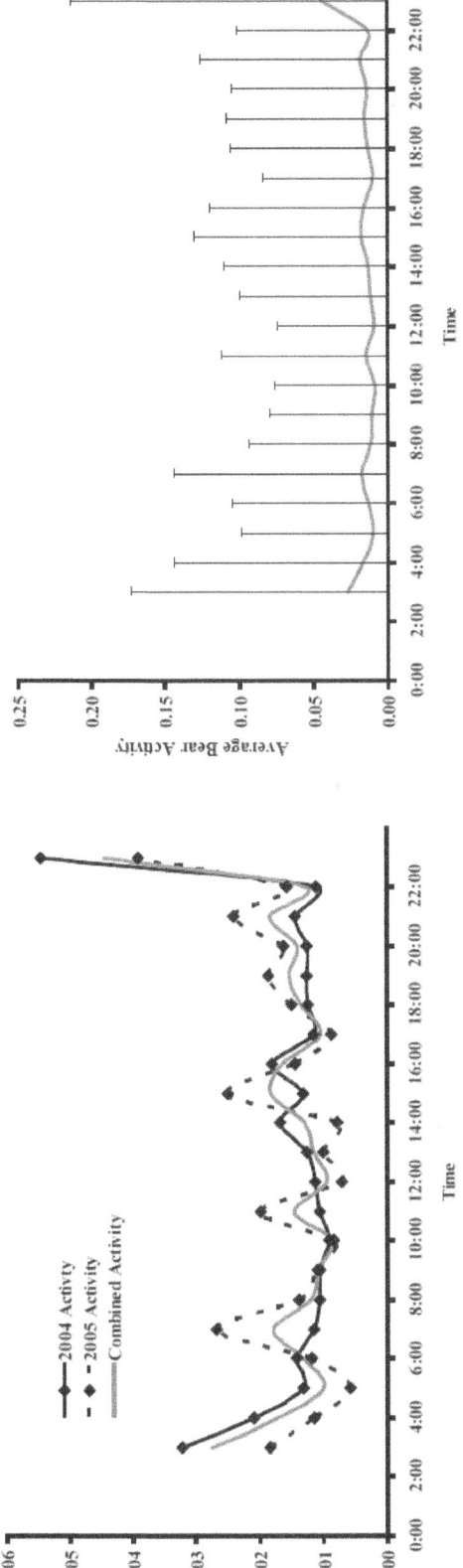

Figure 15. Bear activity rate by time of day.

39

Table 1. Seasonal categories for camera, scat, and hair data.

Tape #

	1	2	3	4	5	6
Johns Hopkins	6/2 – 6/13	6/15 – 6/25	6/29 – 7/10	7/13 – 7/24	7/27 – 8/6	8/10 – 8/20
Queen Inlet	6/2 – 6/14	6/14 – 6/24	6/28 – 7/8	7/13 – 7/24	7/26 – 8/2	8/9 – 8/20
Reid Inlet	6/4 – 6/14	6/16 – 6/26	6/29 – 7/9	7/13 – 7/25	7/28 – 8/8	8/11 – 8/18
Russell Passage	6/5 – 6/15	N/A	6/30 – 7/11	7/15 – 7/24	7/30 – 8/9	8/11 – 8/23
Sandy Cove	6/6 – 6/16	6/17 – 6/28	7/2 – 7/12	7/17 – 7/27	7/31 – 8/15	8/13 – 8/25
Tarr Inlet	6/2 – 6/12	6/15 – 6/25	6/29 – 7/10	7/12 – 7/24	7/27 – 8/7	8/10 – 8/20
Tlingit Point	6/6 – 6/16	6/17 – 6/27	7/2 – 7/8	7/17 – 7/27	7/31 – 8/5	8/14 – 8/24
Wolf Point	6/3 – 6/12	6/15 – 6/25	6/30 – 7/10	7/14 – 7/24	7/28 – 8/7	8/11 – 8/17
	Early/Mid June	Mid/Late June	Late June/Mid July	Mid/Late July	Late July/Mid August	Mid/Late August

Collection Trip #

	2	3	4	5	6	7
Johns Hopkins	6/2 – 6/15	6/15 – 6/29	6/29 – 7/13	7/13 – 7/27	7/27 – 8/10	8/10 – 8/25
Queen Inlet	6/2 – 6/14	6/14 – 6/28	6/28 – 7/13	7/13 – 7/26	7/26 – 8/9	8/9 – 8/23
Reid Inlet	6/4 – 6/16	6/16 – 6/29	6/29 – 7/14	7/14 – 7/28	7/28 – 8/11	8/11 – 8/25
Russell Passage	6/5 – 6/16	6/16 – 6/30	6/30 – 7/15	7/15 – 7/29	7/29 – 8/12	8/12 – 8/26
Sandy Cove	6/6 – 6/17	6/17 – 7/2	7/2 – 7/17	7/17 – 7/31	7/31 – 8/14	8/14 – 8/27
Tarr Inlet	6/2 – 6/15	6/15 – 6/29	6/29 – 7/13	7/13 – 7/27	7/27 – 8/10	8/10 – 8/26
Tlingit Point	6/6 – 6/17	6/17 – 7/1	7/1 – 7/16	7/16 – 7/30	7/30 – 8/13	8/13 – 8/27
Wolf Point	6/3 – 6/17	6/17 – 7/2	7/2 – 7/16	7/16 – 7/30	7/30 – 8/13	8/13 – 9/1
	Early/Mid June	Mid/Late June	Late June/Mid July	Mid/Late July	Late July/Mid August	Mid/Late August

Table 2. Percent cover of habitat types and potential plant bear forage species by study site.

Study Site	Halophytic Wet Forb/Graminoid Herbaceous				Bear Food Data		Dry Graminoid Herbaceous		Bear Food Data	
	Area (km²)	% Food Coverage	Area (km²)	% of Study Site	% Coverage	% of Total Food	Area (km²)	% of Study Site	% Coverage	% of Total Food
Russell Passage	0.191	73.1	0.047	24.4	52.8	17.6	0.026	13.8	36.3	6.9
Queen Inlet	0.071	73.1	0.015	20.4	31.5	8.8	0.005	6.6	18.7	1.7
Sandy Cove	0.091	45.1	0.018	19.6	50.7	22.1	0.007	7.3	61.4	9.9
Reid Inlet	0.068	44.7	0.004	6.4	52.1	7.5	0.016	24.2	18.6	10.1
Wolf Point	0.098	22.1	0.037	38.2	44.1	76.2	0.014	14.8	18.5	12.3
Tarr Inlet	0.041	23.7					0.009	20.8	4.3	3.8
Tlingit Point	0.030	21.6					0.006	19.4	14.0	12.5
Johns Hopkins Inlet	0.024	7.1					0.003	13.1	0.6	1.1
Average				21.8	46.2	26.4		15.0	21.6	7.3
StdDev				11.4	8.9	28.5		6.2	19.4	4.6

41

Table 2. Percent cover of habitat types and bear forage by study site.—Continued

Study Site	Low Open Scrub Area (km²)	% Food Coverage	Low Open Scrub Bear Food Data Area (km²)	% of Study Site	% Coverage	% of Total Food	Wet Graminoid Herbaceous (a) Bear Food Data Area (km²)	% of Study Site	% Coverage	% of Total Food
Russell Passage	0.191	73.1	0.064	33.7	105.9	48.8	0.001	0.5	68.0	0.5
Queen Inlet	0.071	73.1	0.017	23.3	93.5	29.8				
Sandy Cove	0.091	45.1	0.008	9.1	60.3	12.2	0.004	4.3	76.4	0.2
Reid Inlet	0.068	44.7	0.013	19.5	31.3	13.7				
Wolf Point	0.098	22.1	0.006	6.4	10.2	3.0				
Tarr Inlet	0.041	23.7	0.004	8.5	21.3	7.7				
Tlingit Point	0.030	21.6	0.005	15.7	52.7	38.4				
Johns Hopkins Inlet	0.024	7.1	0.015	62.7	2.8	24.8				
Average				**22.4**	**47.3**	**22.3**		**2.4**	**72.2**	**0.3**
StdDev				**18.6**	**37.9**	**16.0**				

Table 2. Percent cover of habitat types and bear foods by study site. —Continued

| | Wet Graminoid Herbaceous (b) | | | | | | Closed Tall Scrub | | | |
| | | | Bear Food Data | | | | Bear Food Data | | | |
Study Site	Area (km²)	% Food Coverage	Area (km²)	% of Study Site	% Coverage	% of Total Food	Area (km²)	% of Study Site	% Coverage	% of Total Food
Russell Passage	0.191	73.1					0.053	27.5	70.1	26.3
Queen Inlet	0.071	73.1					0.035	49.7	87.9	59.7
Sandy Cove	0.091	45.1	0.002	1.7	86.8	0.2				
Reid Inlet	0.068	44.7					0.032	47.2	63.1	66.5
Wolf Point	0.098	22.1					0.040	40.6	4.8	8.5
Tarr Inlet	0.041	23.7					0.029	70.7	29.6	88.5
Tlingit Point	0.030	21.6								
Johns Hopkins Inlet	0.024	7.1					0.006	24.2	21.9	74.2
Average				1.7	86.8	0.2		43.3	46.2	53.9
StdDev								16.9	32.2	30.4

43

Table 2. Percent cover of habitat types and bear foods by study site. —Continued

Study Site	Dry Forb Herbaceous Area (km²)	% Food Coverage	Bear Food Data Area (km²)	% of Study Site	% Coverage	% of Total Food	Closed Needle leaf Forest Bear Food Data Area (km²)	% of Study Site	% Coverage	% of Total Food
Russell Passage	0.191	73.1								
Queen Inlet	0.071	73.1								
Sandy Cove	0.091	45.1					0.053	58.0	43.1	55.4
Reid Inlet	0.068	44.7	0.002	2.6	37.6	2.2				
Wolf Point	0.098	22.1								
Tarr Inlet	0.041	23.7								
Tlingit Point	0.030	21.6					0.019	64.9	16.4	49.1
Johns Hopkins Inlet	0.024	7.1								
Average				2.6	37.6	2.2		61.4	29.8	52.2
StdDev										

44

Table 3. Percent cover of forage species by habitat type.

A) Halophytic Wet Forb/Graminoid Herbaceous

Species	# of Study Sites Found In	Coverage	
		Average	StdDev
Plantago maritima	5	21.3	8.9
Puccinellia nutkaensis	5	18.9	6.9
Carex spp.	2	8.6	N/A
Elymus arenarius	4	1.6	0.9
Triglochin maritima	4	1.1	1.0
Unknown Graminoid	3	0.7	0.4
Oxytropis campestris	1	0.2	N/A
Astragulus spp.	1	0.0	N/A
Fragaria chiloensis	1	0.0	N/A

B) Dry Graminoid Herbaceous

Species	# of Study Sites Found In	Coverage	
		Average	StdDev
Elymus arenarius	7	15.7	16.3
Plantago maritima	7	4.6	4.9
Lathyrus maritima	2	2.3	N/A
Fragaria chiloensis	4	1.9	2.9
Puccinellia nutkaensis	3	1.8	2.4
Carex spp.	1	1.7	N/A
Angelica spp.	1	1.0	N/A
Unknown Graminoid	8	0.8	1.2
Conioselium chinense	1	0.5	N/A
Shepherdia canadensis	1	0.5	N/A
Astagulus spp.	3	0.3	0.2
Barbarea orthoceras	1	0.2	N/A
Oxytropis campestris	1	0.2	N/A
Rubus arctica	1	0.2	N/A
Triglochin maritima	2	0.2	N/A
Equisetum spp.	2	0.1	N/A
Heracleum lanatum	2	0.1	N/A
Ligusticum hultenii	2	0.1	N/A
Rubus spectabilis	1	0.0	N/A
Taraxacum spp.	1	0.0	N/A

Table 3. Percent cover of forage species by habitat type.—Continued

C) Low Open Scrub

Species	# of Study Sites Found In	Coverage Average	StdDev
Fragaria chiloensis	6	17.6	16.2
Shepherdia canadensis	6	10.7	9.3
Astragalus spp.	5	7.3	6.8
Elymus arenarius	7	5.1	5.2
Unknown Graminoid	7	5.0	4.3
Oxytropis campestris	3	4.8	5.9
Lathyrus maritima	3	3.9	6.3
Angelica spp.	2	3.2	N/A
Heracleum lanatum	3	3.1	3.1
Arctostaphylos uva-ursi	5	2.2	1.7
Plantago maritima	4	2.2	2.2
Rubus arctica	1	2.2	N/A
Equisetum spp.	5	2.1	2.6
Carex spp.	8	1.8	3.2
Lupinus spp.	1	1.7	N/A
Athyrium felix-femina	1	1.0	N/A
Rubus spectabilis	1	0.9	N/A
Conioselium chinense	5	0.8	0.7
Taraxacum spp.	4	0.8	0.8
Actea rubra	1	0.6	N/A
Hedysarum alpinum	2	0.4	N/A
Ligusticum hultenii	2	0.2	N/A
Triglochin spp.	1	0.2	N/A
Puccinellia nutkaensis	1	0.1	N/A
Barbarea orthoceras	1	0.0	N/A
Boshniakia rossica	1	0.0	N/A

Table 3. Percent cover of forage species by habitat type.—Continued

D) Dry Forb/Wet Graminoid Herbaceous

Species	# of Study Sites Found In	Coverage Average	StdDev
Carex spp.	2	35.8	N/A
Equisetum spp.	1	26.5	N/A
Unknown Graminoid	3	10.9	7.9
Astragalus spp.	2	5.6	N/A
Plantago maritima	3	4.6	3.2
Triglochin maritima	2	3.8	N/A
Elymus arenarius	3	3.7	3.6
Fragaria chiloensis	3	2.5	1.5
Oxytropis campestris	1	1.8	N/A
Rubus arctica	1	1.8	N/A
Hedysarum alpinum	1	1.7	N/A
Taraxacum spp.	2	0.8	N/A
Heracleum lanatum	1	0.6	N/A
Rubus spectabilis	1	0.6	N/A
Ligusticum hultenii	1	0.5	N/A
Conioselium chinense	1	0.4	N/A
Athyrium filix-femina	1	0.3	N/A
Lathyrus maritima	1	0.1	N/A
Actea rubra	1	0.0	N/A

E) Closed Tall Scrub

Species	# of Study Sites Found In	Coverage Average	StdDev
Shepherdia canadensis	6	27.1	17.7
Fragaria chiloensis	2	14.5	N/A
Unknown Graminoid	5	3.9	4.4
Equisetum spp.	5	3.7	2.9
Astagulus spp.	4	3.6	2.0
Arctostaphylos uva-ursi	5	2.7	4.7
Hedysarum alpinum	2	1.7	N/A
Elymus arenarius	5	1.2	1.1
Oxytropis campestris	3	0.9	1.3
Carex spp.	5	0.7	0.4
Angelica spp.	1	0.5	N/A
Conioselium chinense	2	0.5	N/A
Actea rubra	1	0.4	N/A
Heracleum lanatum	2	0.4	N/A
Rubus arctica	1	0.4	N/A
Vaccinium spp.	1	0.4	N/A
Athyrium felix-femina	2	0.1	N/A
Taraxacum spp.	2	0.1	N/A

Table 3. Percent cover of forage species by habitat type.—Continued

F) Closed Needle leaf Forest

Species	# of Study Sites Found In	Coverage Average	StdDev
Oplopanax horridus	1	16.6	N/A
Rubus spectabilis	1	10.1	N/A
Unknown Graminoid	2	2.7	N/A
Equisetum spp.	2	2.5	N/A
Fragaria chiloensis	2	2.0	N/A
Streptopus amplexifolius	2	1.7	N/A
Lathyrus maritimus	1	1.5	N/A
Angelica spp.	1	1.3	N/A
Elymus arenarius	2	1.2	N/A
Aruncus dioicus	1	1.1	N/A
Conioselium chinense	2	1.0	N/A
Actea rubra	2	0.8	N/A
Athyrium felix-femina	1	0.8	N/A
Carex spp.	2	0.5	N/A
Heracleum lanatum	1	0.5	N/A
Astragalus spp.	1	0.4	N/A
Osmorhiza chilensis	2	0.4	N/A
Rubus pedatus	1	0.4	N/A
Boshniakia rossica	2	0.2	N/A
Rubus arctica	1	0.2	N/A
Taraxacum spp.	1	0.1	N/A
Triglochin maritima	1	0.1	N/A

Table 4. Results of bear sign mapping.

Study Site	Scats	Hair Samples	Rub Trees	Chew Logs	Bear Beds
Sandy Cove	239	74	6	3	6
Queen Inlet	116	225	9	2	7
Russell Passage	163	141	6	3	6
Tlingit Point	10	56	5	1	2
Reid Inlet	44	126	8	1	8
Tarr Inlet	16	26	5	1	2
Wolf Point	33	59	5	0	24
Johns Hopkins	4	20	0	0	0

Table 5. Collection and DNA analysis data for hair samples encountered in 2005.

Study Site	Total Samples Collected	Samples Submitted	Individual Identification	Frequency	%
Johns Hopkins Inlet	7	5	Successful	3	60.00
			Unsuccessful	2	40.00
Queen Inlet	92	72	Successful	35	48.61
			Unsuccessful	37	51.39
Reid Inlet	43	35	Successful	21	60.00
			Unsuccessful	14	40.00
Russell Passage	77	59	Successful	25	42.37
			Unsuccessful	34	57.63
Sandy Cove	45	32	Successful	21	65.63
			Unsuccessful	11	34.37
Tarr Inlet	14	8	Successful	2	25.00
			Unsuccessful	6	75.00
Tlingit Point	40	28	Successful	18	62.07
			Unsuccessful	10	37.93
Wolf Point	38	25	Successful	18	72.00
			Unsuccessful	7	28.00
Total	**356**	**264**			

Table 6. DNA analysis success for hair samples by collection source.

Source	Individual Identification	Frequency	% of Source
Barb Tree	Successful	25	56.82
	Unsuccessful	19	43.18
Chew Log	Successful	23	53.49
	Unsuccessful	20	46.51
Hair Trap	Successful	37	63.79
	Unsuccessful	21	36.21
opportunistic	Successful	2	22.22
	Unsuccessful	7	77.78
Rub Tree	Successful	56	50.91
	Unsuccessful	54	49.09
Total		**264**	

Table 7. Numbers, species, and sex of individuals identified with genetic testing by study site.

Study Site	*Ursus arctos*		*Ursus americanus*		Total
	Male	Female	Male	Female	
Russell Passage	6	7	0	0	13
Queen Inlet	2	7	0	0	9
Sandy Cove	0	0	6	2	8
Reid Inlet	6	0	0	0	6
Tlingit Point	1	0	3	2	6
Johns Hopkins	0	2	0	0	2
Wolf Point	2	0	0	0	2
Tarr Inlet	1	0	0	0	1
Total	**18**	**16**	**9**	**4**	**47**

Table 8. Number of times individual bears were identified by study site.

Study Site	Species	Sex	n	Times Identified		# of Sources		# of Trips Identified	
				Mean	StdDev	Mean	StdDev	Mean	StdDev
Johns Hopkins	*U. arctos*	Female	2	1.5	N/A	1	N/A	1	N/A
Queen Inlet	*U. arctos*	Both	9	3.78	3.38	2.33	1.66	1.56	0.73
	U. arctos	Male	2	2.5	N/A	2	N/A	1.5	N/A
	U. arctos	Female	7	4.14	3.80	2.33	1.66	1.56	0.79
Reid Inlet	*U. arctos*	Male	6	3.50	3.15	2.00	1.26	1.17	0.41
Russell Passage	*U. arctos*	Both	13	1.92	1.80	1.54	1.45	1.31	0.63
	U. arctos	Male	5	2.83	2.40	2.17	2.04	1.67	0.82
	U. arctos	Female	7	1.14	0.38	1.00	0.00	1.00	0.00
Sandy Cove	*U. americanus*	Both	8	2.63	1.69	1.38	0.74	1.63	0.74
	U. americanus	Male	6	1.83	0.75	1.17	0.41	1.20	0.52
	U. americanus	Female	2	5.00	N/A	2.50	N/A	2.50	N/A
Tarr Inlet	*U. arctos*	Male	1	2	N/A	2	N/A	1	N/A
Tlingit Point	*U. arctos*	Male	1	1	N/A	1	N/A	1	N/A
	U. americanus	Both	3	3.40	1.52	1.80	0.84	1.60	0.55
	U. americanus	Male	3	2.67	0.58	1.33	0.58	1.33	0.58
	U. americanus	Female	2	4.5	N/A	2.5	N/A	2	N/A
Wolf Point	*U. arctos*	Male	2	9.00	N/A	3.00	N/A	1.50	N/A

Table 9. Remote camera data by study site.

Study Site	2004		2005		Total Camera Days
	Tapes Collected	Camera Days	Tapes Collected	Camera Days	
Johns Hopkins	1 – 4	38.50	1 – 6	58.18	**96.68**
Queen Inlet	1 – 6	57.96	1 – 6	53.68	**111.64**
Reid Inlet	1 – 6	52.43	3 – 6	30.83	**83.25**
Russell Passage	1, 3 – 6	45.70	3 – 6	28.92	**74.62**
Sandy Cove	1 – 3, 5 – 6	41.72	1 – 6	58.26	**99.98**
Tarr Inlet	1 – 6	53.81	1 – 6	57.83	**111.64**
Tlingit Point	1 – 6	50.05	None	0.00	**50.05**
Wolf Point	1 - 6	53.81	None	0.00	**53.81**
	Total	**393.98**		**287.70**	**681.67**

Table 10. Bear activity data from remote camera units. Activity reported is a ratio of total number of video frames with bears present divided by the total number of video frames recorded.

Year	Study Site	Bear Activity		Bear Minutes in Site	
		Average	StdDev	Average	Maximum
2004	Johns Hopkins	0.011	0.08	13.24	103.53
2004	Queen Inlet	0.042	0.18	50.00	268.16
2004	Reid Inlet	0.004	0.05	4.21	59.95
2004	Russell Passage	0.003	0.03	4.07	43.54
2004	Sandy Cove	0.041	0.15	49.09	224.67
2004	Tarr Inlet	0.009	0.08	11.09	109.66
2004	Tlingit Point	0.001	0.01	0.68	10.50
2004	Wolf Point	0.004	0.05	4.83	66.60
2004 Total		**0.014**	**0.10**	**16.27**	**131.33**
2004 Total w/o TL & WO		0.018	0.11	21.28	152.95
2005	Johns Hopkins	0.002	0.02	2.37	28.62
2005	Queen Inlet	0.040	0.17	48.29	254.93
2005	Reid Inlet	0.004	0.04	4.80	50.55
2005	Russell Passage	0.007	0.04	7.86	61.04
2005	Sandy Cove	0.026	0.11	30.82	160.46
2005	Tarr Inlet	0.002	0.04	2.02	52.22
2005 Total		**0.014**	**0.09**	**17.38**	**131.26**
Grand Total		**0.014**	**0.10**	**16.74**	**131.30**

Table 11. Combined bear minutes data from remote camera units by study site.

Site	Bear Activity		Bear Minutes	
	Average	StdDev	Average/day	Maximum/day
Queen Inlet	0.041	0.18	49	264
Sandy Cove	0.032	0.12	38	186
Russell Passage	0.005	0.04	6	52
Tarr Inlet	0.005	0.06	6	84
Johns Hopkins	0.006	0.05	7	68
Wolf Point	0.004	0.05	5	66
Reid Inlet	0.004	0.04	5	58
Tlingit Point	0.001	0.01	1	11

Table 12. Study site ranking data.

Site	Average Activity	Rank	Area Size (km²)	Rank	Bear Foods Food Coverage (m²)	Rank	Forage Diversity Index	Rank	Collections Scats/Field Day	Rank	Hair/Field Day	Rank	# Bears	Rank	Ave Rank[a]
Queen Inlet	0.041	1	0.071	4	51942.35	2	0.68	4	0.73	3	1.39	1	9	2	**2.2**
Sandy Cove	0.032	2	0.091	3	45292.53	3	0.92	1	1.47	1	0.45	4	8	3	**2.3**
Russell Passage	0.005	5	0.191	1	139603.90	1	0.81	2	0.99	2	0.85	2	13	1	**2.2**
Tarr Inlet	0.005	4	0.041	6	9774.37	6	0.54	6	0.09	6	0.15	7	1	8	**6.2**
Johns Hopkins	0.006	3	0.024	8	1698.88	8	0.24	8	0.04	8	0.12	8	2	6	**6.8**
Wolf Point	0.004	6	0.098	2	21696.61	5	0.49	7	0.19	5	0.34	5	2	6	**5.7**
Reid Inlet	0.004	7	0.068	5	30269.24	4	0.68	4	0.27	4	0.76	3	6	4	**4.3**
Tlingit Point	0.001	8	0.030	7	6426.32	7	0.76	3	0.06	7	0.34	6	6	4	**5.8**

[a] Average rank was calculated by summing all rank values for each site and dividing by 6, area size rank excluded.

Shaded cells (Tarr Inlet and Johns Hopkins) are camping closure areas.

Appendix 1. GLBA Bear Habitat Classification

Vegetation Classification to Level III (Viereck and others, 1992)

I. *Woody*

    a) Closed needle leaf forest (I.A.1.)
Canopy cover of 60-100% with >75% of canopy comprised of coniferous trees
Dominated by *Picea* species with *Salix, Alnus* and herbaceous under story.

    b) Closed tall scrub (II.B.1)
Tall (>1.5 meters) shrub cover of >75%
Shrubs dominated by *Salix, Populus* and/or *Alnus* species.

II. *Open Scrub Herb*

    Open low scrub (II.C.2)
Low (0.2-1.5 meters) shrub cover of 25-75%
Shrubs dominated by *Shepherdia, Salix,* or *Alnus* species
Other plant communities present may include dwarf scrub (Dryas), dry or mesic forb herbaceous

III. *Rye*

    Dry graminoid herbaceous (III.A.1.)
Forbs and graminoid species in well drained soils
Dominated by *Elymus arenarius* and/or *Honckenya peploides*

IV. *Halophytic grass-herb*

    Wet graminoid herbaceous (III.A.3)/ Wet forb herbaceous (III.B.3)
Graminoids and forbs occupying wet sites, **halophytic**
Dominated by *Plantago maritima* and/or *Puccinellia nutkaensis*, often with *Triglochin* and/or *Carex* species

V. *Graminoid and Graminoid herb*

    Wet graminoid herbaceous (III.A.3)
Graminoids and forbs occupying wet sites, **not halophytic**
Dominated by *Carex*, other graminoids and/or *Equisetum* species

VI. *Herb*

    Dry forb herbaceous (III.B.1)
Forb communities on dry sites
Dominated by a wide variety of seral and/or mesic herbs

Appendix 2. Data Sheets

I. Collection Data Sheet

GLBA Bear Research Collection Data Sheet

Trip #:   Location: Date: GPS File #:

Trip	Sample #	Description	DNA?	Source	Age	Quality	Comments

Appendix 2. Bear forage phenology data sheet.—Continued

ID	Common Name	Scientific Name	Present	Eaten	Comments
	Forbs				
ACRU	Baneberry	Actea rubra			
ANSP	Sea watch/white angelica	Angelica spp.			
ARUV	Bearberry	Arctostaphylos uva-ursi			
ARDI	Goatsbeard	Aruncus dioicus			
ASSP	Vetch	Astragulus spp			
ATFI	Lady Fern	Athyrium felix-femina			
BAOR	American Wintercress	Barbarea orthoceras			
BORO	Groundcone	Boschniakia rossica			
COCH	Pacific Hemlock-Parsley	Conioselium chinense			
EQSP	Horsetail	Equisetum spp.			
FRCH	Strawberry	Fragaria chiloensis			
HEAL	Alpine Sweetvetch	Hedysarum alpinum			
HELA	Cow Parsnip	Heracleum lanatum			
LAMA	Beach Pea	Lathyrus maritimus			
LIHU	Beach Lovage	Ligusticum hultenii			
LUSP	Lupine	Lupinus spp.			
OPHO	Devil's Club	Oplopanax horridus			
OSDE	Licorice Root	Osmorhiza chilensis			
OXCA	Field Oxytrope	Oxytropis campestris			
PLMA	Goose Tongue	Plantago maritima			
RISP	Currant	Ribes spp.			
RUAR	Nagoonberry	Rubus arctica			
RUSP	Salmonberry	Rubus spectabilis			
SARA	Red-elderberry	Sambucus racemosa			
SHCA	Soapberry	Shepherdia canadensis			
STAM	Twisted Stalk	Streptopus amplexifolius			
TASP	Dandelion	Taraxacum spp.			
TRMA	Sea Arrow-Grass	Triglochin maritimum			
VASP	Blueberry/Huckleberry	Vaccinium spp.			
VIED	High-bush Cranberry	Viburnum edule			

Appendix 2. Bear forage phenology data sheet.—Continued

Grasses

ELAR	Rye-grass	*Elymus arenarius*
CASP	Sedges	*Carex* spp.
PUNU	Pacific Alkaligrass	*Puccinellia nutkaensis*
UNGR	Unknown graminoid	N/A

Animals

BASP	Barnacles	*Balanus* spp.
MYED	Blue Mussels	*Mytilus edulis*
ONSP	Salmon	*Onchorynchus* spp.
	Other Animal (Specify)	

Appendix 3. Phenological classifications and definitions.

A) Present (PR): Restricted to animal food items to simply denote presence/absence.

B) Vegetative (VE): Plants are actively growing or phenology is difficult to determine.

C) Early Flower (EF): Plants are in early stages of flowering.

D) Flower (FL): Plants have mature flowers

E) Late Flower (LF): Plants still have mature flowers but some seeds (or berries) are starting to form.

F) Early Seed (ES): Similar to late flower with the addition of more immature seeds or berries formed.

G) Seed (SE): Plants have fully mature seeds or berries.

H) Late Seed (LS): Seeds and berries are starting to drop or die.

I) Dead or Dying (DE): Plant is wilting, browning, and start to die.

J) No Data (-): Species was not noticed during a particular field visit or data was not recorded.

www.ingramcontent.com/pod-product-compliance
Lightning Source LLC
Chambersburg PA
CBHW080436290526
45791CB00008BA/2516